Raging Like a Fire

RAGING LIKE A FIRE

A Celebration
of Irving Layton

EDITED BY HENRY BEISSEL & JOY BENNETT

Published in collaboration with Concordia University

Véhicule Press

MONTRÉAL

Thank you to the Irving Layton Collection, Concordia University for providing invaluable assistance. Permission to reproduce letter from Jack McClelland to Irving Layton (17 January 1957) courtesy of Jack McClelland. Quotations from Raymond Souster's letters (which appear in *Adjusting the Sights,* courtesy of the author. Ann Diamond's "Layton at Eighty" first appeared in the *Montreal Gazette,* 7 March 1992; Nancy-Gay Rotstein's "Greatness" first appeared in *Taking Off* (Longman Canada, 1979); David Solway's "Framing Layton" first appeared in *Matrix* (November 1992); and Andy Wainwright's 'The One-Eyed Man" first appeared in *The Requiem Journals* (Fiddlehead Poetry Books, 1976).

Published with the assistance of The Canada Council.

Cover design: Mark Garland
Cover photo of Irving Layton: Sam Tata
Photo of cover artwork: Michel Filion
Frontispiece drawing: Sharon Katz
Design and imaging: ECW Type & Art
Printing: Imprimerie d'Édition Marquis Ltée

CANADIAN CATALOGUING IN PUBLICATION DATA

Main entry under title:
   Raging like a fire : a celebration of Irving Layton

ISBN 1-55065-042-4 (bound) –
ISBN 1-55065-040-8 (pbk.)

1. Layton, Irving, 1912– — Criticism and interpretation.
I. Beissel, Henry, 1929– . II. Bennett, Joy, 1946– .

PS8523.A95Z83 1993   C811'.54   C93-090132-0
PR9199.3.L39Z83 1993

Véhicule Press, P.O.B. 125, Place du Parc Station, Montreal,
Quebec H2W 2M9

Distributed in Canada by General Distribution Services, 30 Lesmill Road, Don Mills, Ontario M3B 2T6, and in the United States by Inbook/Inland Book Company, Inc., East Haven, CT 06512.

Printed in Canada on acid-free paper.

CONTENTS

INTRODUCTION

This book is a *Festschrift* — which means that the reader is invited to a literary party. For this party, poets, scholars and friends have come together to celebrate the 80th birthday of one of Canada's major poets: Irving Layton! And the party takes place at Concordia University because Irving has had a long and rich relationship with the university.

Irving first taught at what was then Sir George Williams College in the 1950s. When the College became Sir George Williams University he joined us as lecturer and writer-in-residence, primarily to teach poetry. After a sojourn in Toronto during the 1970s, where he taught at York University, he returned to what had meanwhile become Concordia University, initially as writer-in-residence to our Creative Writing Program, and, more recently, as Adjunct Professor in the English Department.

Of the many tributes paid to Irving in this book, none are more deserved than those by former students who celebrate him for his selfless dedication as a teacher: he cajoled and provoked them, encouraged, inspired, challenged them, and always had time for them individually when they sought his council or needed consolation. So exceptional was his contribution as a teacher that the Creative Writing Program decided to honour him by establishing the annual Irving Layton Awards for Creative Writing, one each in poetry and fiction, for undergraduate students, to the funding of which the proceeds from the sale of this book are committed.

There is yet another important relationship between Irving and Concordia: the prestigious Irving Layton Collection. Begun with a few boxes of manuscripts and correspondence in 1969, the Layton Collection has now grown to a very large and very important archive of over 500 manuscripts, several thousand pieces of correspondence from over 300 correspondents, ten personal notebooks, five scrapbooks, audio and video tapes, thousands of clippings, photographs, and published works. This collection is a cornerstone of the Concordia University Library's special collections, and has drawn numerous scholars and researchers to the university. It is an on-going commitment that includes, among recent additions, the manuscript of *Waiting for the Messiah*, Layton's autobiography.

All of this, we felt, added up to a powerful bond that called for a suitable celebration on the occasion of Irving's 80th birthday. Besides, we Canadians are too bashful about celebrating our artists, and it is high time that we learned to pay tribute to them publicly when and where tribute is due — and it is certainly due Irving Layton. Given his colourful and courageous personality, it is inevitable that Irving's reputation is not without controversy. The *Festschrift*, while honouring him, is intended to open new vistas into Irving the man and the poet, and perhaps clear up some misconceptions about him. Naturally, the editors don't necessarily identify with every opinion expressed by the contributors; but what matters is that all of us have joined together to celebrate one of Canada's finest poets, and to wish him many more years of that "wild peculiar joy" where life and poetry become one.

Henry Beissel *&* Joy Bennett

THE IMPORTANCE OF KNOWING IRVING: A MEMOIR, IN LIEU OF A BIOGRAPHY

Roy MacSkimming

Fifteen years ago I was to be Irving Layton's biographer. Like most events that *might* have happened, this one has little significance except as a matter for speculation: what sort of biography would have resulted, had I assumed the task in place of Elspeth Cameron? What would its impact have been on Layton's reputation?

Not that I've asked him, but Layton himself would no doubt contend I should have proceeded full speed ahead with the project back in 1977; and not only that, I should still consider writing the book, even now. It would be his opinion that there's plenty of room for other lives of Layton (he has, after all, led many lives); moreover, he has continued to live and love and write and produce new material for his biographers since the appearance of Cameron's *Irving Layton: A Portrait* in 1985. Certainly she should not have the last word — and will not, as the present volume attests.

For the record, that unwritten biography was conceived in a country cottage on the island of Mallorca, where my wife and children and I spent nine impoverishing months amid superb natural beauty in 1976-77. As our funds dwindled and our sense of isolation increased, the need for a substantial and at least semi-commercial writing project became compelling: one that would restore a broken connection with home, while generating some needed income. (At that point I had worked ten years in Canadian book publishing, two as literary editor and columnist for *The Toronto Star*, and had temporarily retired to write a second novel.) There was even a certain appropriateness to a Mallorca-Layton connection. During Layton's intense literary correspondence with the American poet Robert Creeley in the mid-1950s, Creeley had been living on Mallorca; Layton, already feeling the need for warmer, more sensual landscapes which would eventually take him to Spain, Italy and especially Greece, had written Creeley asking what it would cost to rent a house on the island.

In any case, in the middle of winter 1977 I made a brief trip from Mallorca to Toronto, where Layton was then living with his third wife, Aviva, to sound him out on the project. We discussed it over dinner with Aviva and their son, David. Irving was distinctly pleased—he knew my high opinion of his work — and offered his wholehearted encouragement and cooperation. Others, such as Wynne Francis, had talked of doing a biography, and he'd encouraged them also; but for the moment, he assured me, the field was wide open. Predictably enough, he agreed with my assessment that the time had come for telling his remarkable story as man and poet and social *agent provocateur*. At the time, CanLit was just beginning to generate momentum as a growth industry, and a full-scale biography of a living Canadian writer was a relatively new idea; the boldness of the concept appealed to both of us. By the end of the evening we agreed that my next step was to approach Layton's longtime publisher, Jack McClelland, to obtain a commitment.

Jack was interested enough to spend a Saturday morning discussing the project at his home in Forest Hill. He thought the book could be a literary *cause célèbre*, but not likely a bestseller; although he was willing to discuss a contract and advance, the money wouldn't be sufficient, he suspected, to finance the whole research and writing time. He advised me to explore funding possibilities at the granting councils, but first to meet with his editor-in-chief, Anna Porter, to obtain a second opinion. After Anna confirmed Jack's estimate of the book's market, and the consequent limitations on M&S's financial commitment, I visited The Canada Council in Ottawa.

The head of the Council's Writing and Publishing Section, Naim Kattan, agreed that the project would be eligible for funding, should a jury decide to recommend it. But Kattan seemed eager to put that question aside and discuss another matter of greater interest to him. A key position on his staff for a granting officer in charge of book publishing programs had become vacant; the Council was having difficulty finding a qualified candidate — someone with publishing experience at a senior level and knowledge of the English-Canadian literary scene. Would I be interested?

The next thing I knew, I was sitting in the office of the Council's Associate Director, Timothy Porteous, being casually but rather determinedly interviewed for the position. It was a bizarre sensation: to travel the cultural distance from a Spanish almond grove to a mandarin's office high above Ottawa in the middle of a swirling January snowstorm, and to be offered a job it had never occurred to me to seek.

I travelled back to Mallorca in a state of considerable ambivalence — still excited about the Layton book, but realizing it would be a long-term, unpredictably funded project, which could easily, after a certain point, start costing money I didn't have. With two young sons and an uncertain future economically, could I really afford to take it on? The Canada Council position, on the other hand, offered financial and professional stability, as well as a ticket back home. After talking it over with my family, I opted for reason over passion and accepted the Council's offer — an un-Laytonic decision in more ways than one.

For a while I kept alive the hope that I could work on the biography in my spare time. It was a hope shared by Layton, to judge from a letter he wrote me on March 12, 1977: "I'm relieved, no, delighted that you're still interested in the project. I can't think of anyone else into whose hands I'd more willingly put my obsessions." But as it turned out, 'spare time' from my Canada Council work was practically non-existent. Four years later, according to Elspeth Cameron, Layton approached her to become his biographer.

Since then, witnessing the public acrimony between them over *Irving Layton: A Portrait*, I've often thought: there but for the grace of God go I. However immaterial it may be in the circumstances, I suspect I would have written a very different book from Cameron's — not better, perhaps not nearly as good, just different — if only because of differences in our personalities, sensibilities and life-experience. Biography remains, after all, a highly subjective form. To take only one example, her esthetic and critical responses to Layton's poetry (in my view) are tepid, under-engaged, leaning too heavily on the opinions of others. It also appears that her identification with Layton's long-suffering wives led her to fall prey to *parti pris*, to concentrate on his more negative personal qualities while ignoring or at least underestimating his positive ones, with the result that her "portrait" of him is often seriously one-sided.

Had I drawn the portrait, on the other hand, it would have been flawed in other ways — perhaps by excessive bias in the opposite direction, or inadequate knowledge of Jewish culture. Even so, I would have had to address as honestly as I could the selfsame private battlegrounds of Irving's wrecked marriages, inconstant friendships and doomed love affairs, some of which are unflattering to him; and his innumerable literary and political fistfights, in which, as the years wore on, he was increasingly on the wrong side (his support for Lyndon Johnson in Vietnam, his admiration for Richard Nixon). It would have been essential to acknowledge the preposterousness of certain postures he struck, the sometimes outrageous quality of his ego and self-absorption, which could result in hurtful behaviour toward others. But in confronting those character traits, I hope I would have resisted the temptation to set myself up in judgment too quickly. He, or she, who is without sin . . . etc.

Layton is, after all, that extraordinary phenomenon, an original human being: a complex, contrary, compulsively candid artist with an enormous appetite for life and for "knowing other people." One of the difficulties he seems to have posed for Elspeth Cameron was that his mercurial psyche rendered him hopelessly inconsistent in his relationships and public positions; and undisciplined (read not housebroken) in his poetic gift. Or, as Layton once described himself, "By that, by this, by sharp ecstasies perplexed. . . ."

And as Walt Whitman put it, "Do I contradict myself? / Very well then I contradict myself, / (I am large, I contain multitudes.)"

Aside from being the first truly major poet Canada had ever produced, Layton, like Whitman, is also the largest and warmest and most generous of men. Let me try to explain:

In November 1960, I wrote a letter to Layton in Montreal from my home in Ottawa. Fumblingly, and more or less innocently, I tried to express what his poetry meant to me. I was sixteen years old.

By that time I had begun to read widely in the poetry of the sixteenth and seventeenth and nineteenth centuries, but until I discovered *A Red Carpet for the Sun*, I hadn't known a poet who could 'utter for me' — whose work I could enter as I entered my own dreams. That revelation was blinding: I have experienced nothing similar, except in love, ever since. And it was certainly love I felt for Layton's work, for his gift of a contemporary idiom of vivid symbolic utterance. His poems were not only deeply sensual, a musical and 'physical' pleasure to read out loud, but permitted the expression of heretofore inexpressible (for me) perceptions and longings and emotions, in a numinous language that invited endless re-reading. Layton was intoxication.

I have no idea how I phrased it in my letter, but that's how I felt at the time. As a postscript, I ventured the suggestion that I'd like to meet him some day, maybe even visit him in Montreal.

To my astonishment — the prospect of a reply from such a lofty source didn't seem likely — a letter came back almost by return mail, written in fountain-pen in Layton's small, Italianate hand: I was welcome to visit him at home on a certain Saturday the following month. If I arrived in the afternoon, would I care to stay for dinner?

Visiting Layton was a turning point for me. The afternoon in Montreal was a series of surprises. The man himself was considerably shorter than I'd expected, a good four inches shorter than me, yet burly and powerfully built (he'd been a boxer in college). Fixing me with his magnetic, deep-set eyes (although blue, they were very dark), he made me feel, instantly, as if I were just the fellow he'd been wanting to see for a very long time. He settled me in the most comfortable chair in his study-cum-living-room, close to a portrait photograph of George Bernard Shaw, and we began to talk.

I'd never seen so many books in a home before, covering the walls from floor to ceiling; it was like living inside the stacks in a library. And yet the place was much smaller and more modest than I'd imagined, a cramped walk-up apartment on Somerled Avenue in Notre-Dame-de-Grace — practically humble compared to his poetic landscapes, or my mental image of him composing his work in some airy spacious residence. I'd also imagined Layton would do all the talking — about poetry, love, his past, anything — and I'd listen, hoping I could remember it all so I could tell my teenage poet-friends back home and, especially, my girlfriend. Instead, he made *me* talk. He seemed to want to know all about who I was, what my family was like, what I thought about things, whether I was in love. Did I write myself, by any chance? To my mixed horror and delight, I found myself telling him precious secrets of my inner life, then extracting the dozen or so sheets of poems I'd concealed in the breast pocket of my jacket, not believing an opportune moment would ever arrive to produce them, and suddenly wishing it hadn't.

Layton took the poems from my hand and began reading them, while I tried not to squirm too much in the enormous chair. He read every damn one of them.

"This is good," he said finally, matter-of-factly. "Strong stuff. You're a poet, you know. The genuine article."

And suddenly, I was.

Did Layton say something similar to the literally hundreds of other young poets who came to sit at his feet over the years? I don't know; I assume he always made some attempt to be honest, to discriminate to a degree, in order not to mislead the genuinely talentless; but I'm not sure it matters. As Robert Bly has pointed out more recently, every young man has a deep-seated need for the encouragement and validation of older men, and on that day I was extraordinarily encouraged and validated by Layton.

We went on to discuss what it took to be a poet. It meant living as richly as possible, he explained: not learning about humanity by reading alone, but by reaching out boldly and hungrily for *experience*, and savouring it fully, before distilling it in your work. This simple concept, by now so familiar coming from Layton, was heady stuff for a sixteen-year-old. Its stress on boldness and hunger and *action* went well beyond Wordsworth's emotion recollected in tranquillity.

Nor was being a poet for the fainthearted, the compromising: the true poet had to be singlemindedly dedicated to his art, not just practising it as a sideline, or he'd never realize the potential for greatness. "Look at — ," Layton remarked, referring (with some sympathy) to an eminent colleague. "He's tried to be a poet and professor and family man all at once, and he's failed at all three."

I seized immediately on this idea. It was the perfect justification for my usually suppressed desire to quit school and go out on the road, like Kerouac, in search of experience.

"Not so fast now," Layton shot back. "You'll need an education too! No matter how boring you may find your teachers, you won't go far without a good degree. Take everything you can from reading the authors in your courses, never mind the academic twaddle. *Then* hit the road!"

If my father, the educator, could have heard Layton then, he'd have heaved a great sigh of relief.

Eventually, Aviva appeared. She too was short, but lithe, electric in her vivacity. I was fascinated by her: the sharp brittle Australian accent, the bright darting laughter. God knows how many adolescent poets she'd had to put up with on weekends, but she made me feel just as welcome, as wanted, as Irving did. The wholehearted way she smiled, all the way up into her eyes, was irresistible. I saw why

Layton had fallen in love with her, and actually found myself being drawn into her aura instead of his. Embarrassed, I was almost relieved when she went out to the kitchen, at Layton's suggestion, to get us some red wine.

I'd never tasted wine before that moment. I found the sensation peculiarly flat and sour and unappealing — the only surprise of the visit that wasn't utterly captivating. Even the frozen fish-sticks that Aviva thawed out afterwards and served for supper with mashed potatoes and creamed corn seemed wonderful to me. Sheltered, conventional product of the 1950s middle class that I was, as I listened to their dinner-table conversation, I was struck by what seemed the remarkable acceptance and freedom they extended to each other. I gathered that Layton often went off on long, rambling walks by himself through the city, sometimes staying away from home for hours on end while poems (and relationships?) formed in his head. At another point, Aviva lamented that Irving wouldn't be free to accompany her to a play the next week, and he said, "You needn't go alone — ask Leonard to go with you." Turning to me, he remarked, "There's another young poet you should read, Leonard Cohen — he has a book coming out next spring from M&S. You may like his work even better than mine."

At the end of the evening, Layton gave me something else I still treasure. As I put on my coat to leave, he pulled a book off one of the crowded shelves, a small clothbound volume with beige covers: the New Directions edition of Lawrence's selected poems.

"Have you read D.H. Lawrence?"

I hadn't. He shook my hand warmly, then thrust the book into it, saying he hoped we'd talk again soon. Wandering out into the crisp Montreal night, feeling uncommonly blessed, I opened the gift to the first page. Written in the same small script as his letter were the words, "Irving Layton, Montreal, Que., July 1948."

Looking back on that encounter thirty-two years later, I find the exceptional thing about it — quite apart from its personal significance to me — is that Layton at forty-eight (exactly my age at this moment) took the trouble in the first place to devote seven or eight hours out of his life to a young stranger, whose naïveté, however briefly charming it may have seemed (I'm only guessing), must have been on the whole rather shallow and quite possibly boring. Most adults, artistic or otherwise, wouldn't consider it a profitable way to spend their time. Layton not only did consider it so, but offered many, many others — of all ages and both sexes — this gift of himself, of his open-hearted attention and encouragement, with amazing frequency.

In my own case, the visits to Irving and Aviva were repeated on several occasions into my early twenties. Once, in 1963, my arrival coincided with the premiere of Claude Jutra's first feature film, *A Tout Prendre*. "Mr. and Mrs. Layton and Son" had received an invitation to attend at the request of Leonard Cohen, who had written the film's English subtitles; since Irving's son Max wasn't in town, he and Aviva suggested I accompany them. The invitation said "Black Tie," but Irving didn't own a tux and was damned if he was going to rent one. "I'll go as far as jacket and tie," he said, handing me one of his own old ties, somewhat soiled and out-of-fashion, which didn't even come close to matching the corduroy jacket and sports shirt I was wearing.

Thus attired (but with Aviva looking splendid in a dress she'd bought in Paris, or was it Rome), we arrived at the downtown theatre. *Le tout Montréal* — the francophone political and social elites as well as the artistic community — was pulling up in taxis and shiny black limos and, of course, tuxedos. It was a gala *québecois* cultural event. But thanks to Aviva's foresight, we had brought our engraved invitation for three, and so were able to crash the party with only slight difficulty from the doorman.

In the lobby, Cohen was holding forth in tails and cape and silver-topped cane, surrounded by at least six stunning beauties hanging on his every word. Layton called across the lobby, "Leonard, you rascal! What's up? Who are your friends?"

Cohen darted a worried frown at us and hissed, "Shhh, Irving — speak *French*."

"But Leonard," Irving boomed, "I don't *speak* French!"

Finally settled into our seats in the darkened theatre, we endured a number of congratulatory speeches, then Irving wriggled and sighed restlessly throughout much of the film; although he'd become an avid viewer of European cinema, priding himself on his interpretations of symbolism in Bergman and Fellini, he found Jutra's autobiographical movie tedious.

In the meantime, I had begun attending the University of Toronto. I had given readings of both Layton's and Cohen's work at Hart

House, and was writing the liner notes for a recording, "Irving Layton at Le Hibou." The record had been compiled from tapes of several readings Layton had given at an Ottawa coffee house in 1962 and 1963. Curiously, Cameron's biography contains no reference to the now-historic recording, produced in 1964 by Ottawa poet William Hawkins and released by Harvey Glatt's Posterity Records, with a superb cover drawing by Christopher Wells. The recording documents Layton at the height of his powers as a dramatic and humorous presenter of his own work.

I suppose the cynical would speculate that this was just the kind of payoff Layton was seeking from his ever-widening circle of young admirers. I don't believe it was, however: he was that rare middle-aged man — rare at least in my experience — who actually *enjoyed* young people, who thrived on exposure to their freshness, energy, and sense of hope.

The last time I visited the Somerled Avenue apartment, it was on the eve of another big experience, my departure for a *Wanderjahr* in Europe. I was to board the Cunard liner "Carmania" from Montreal en route to Southampton; Irving and Aviva invited me to sleep overnight in Max's unused room. The next morning, Layton drove me down to the docks and made sure I boarded the right ship — another donation of time and trouble which seems, in retrospect, rather extraordinary. And once again, he pressed one of his books into my hand as a memento: Updike's *Rabbit, Run* in hardcover. This time there was a special inscription:

"To Roy, off on the Great Adventure."

This generosity of his, not material but of the spirit, leads me to my conclusion: Layton was a great teacher not only in the classroom, as generations of his students have attested, but in matters of the heart and soul. This is the Irving Layton that I, and a few thousand other people, have had the pleasure and privilege of knowing and enjoying and learning from. In writing this, I hope to speak for all of them, too.

AN IMPERFECT DEVOTION

Gary Geddes

There is a colourful story about Irving Layton the man, which I might safely relate in the context of this book in his honour. The events took place during his tenure at York University, when he came in late and promptly fell asleep (or pretended to) during a public reading by Margaret Atwood. Some wag placed the two of them side by side at the subsequent dinner, and Layton, between soup and the main course, turned his attention to the rising young star.

"Well, Peggy, you're a fine poet, but you know women are only good for one thing."

Silence. All conversation and mastication at the table stops and heads turn in the direction of these two public figures, who many would describe as the leading poets of their respective generations. The brimming spoon in Atwood's hand shows not the slightest hesitation or uncertainty in its circuit from bowl to mouth. Layton laughs at his own outrageousness.

"Just kidding, Peggy. I like your poetry very much."

"Well, I don't like yours."

I begin with this memorable incident because it is, in many ways, typical of Layton's public persona and the controversy that surrounds his work. The gifted but insecure poet, trying to gain control of a public situation where he feels at a slight disadvantage, resorts to verbal pugilism. While Layton's confrontational style worked initially to draw attention to the man and his work, in later years it has had the reverse effect: recognition gives way to notoriety and the poet proves to be an unreliable ambassador for his own poems, many of which consist of adolescent sexual posturing and resort to shock effects, cheap shots, and partisan cliches.

I deeply regret this situation, for which Canada is perhaps as much to blame. As the painter A.Y. Jackson once said, Canadians would rather support a boa constrictor than a poet; he also said that an artist, to survive in Canada, had to become an institution. Or a comedian, he might have added. It seems not enough for a poet to produce brilliant work in this country; he or she must also offer up the life to the insatiable appetites of a media and public that do not understand or care about the nature of artistic inspiration, and its sources in privacy and solitude. I said twenty years ago, when I included Layton's poems in *15 Canadian Poets*, that his real power lies in those poems dealing with the mysteries of the natural world, with the creative process, and with the joys, guilt, and losses of family life. I still hold that view. Layton's an elegist, perhaps our best, and has produced an impressive body of some twenty or so poems that we will always read and cherish. I am thinking here of poems such as "The Swimmer," "The Cold Green Element," "Berry Picking," "Sacrament by the Water," "Whatever Else Poetry is Freedom," "Cain," "Keine Lazarovitch," "A Song for Naomi," and "A Tall Man Executes a Jig," Layton's successful effort to overcome the anxiety of influence produced by the odes of his Romantic forebears and A.M. Klein's "Portrait of the Poet As Landscape."

Although there may be only a few younger poets who would give an arm to have written one of these poems, there are none who can ignore them. Patrick Lane learned his use of the long line from Layton; David Solway has married Layton's prosody to Klein's vocabulary; the shy and awkward Al Purdy found in Layton a domestic naturalism and a comic / nostalgic public persona that he could emulate. Even as gifted and original a poet as Michael Ondaatje signals his debt to Layton's lines about the "violated grass snake that lugged / its intestines like a small red valise," when he writes in his narrative poem "Peter" of the de-tongued and hamstrung monster moving with "his legs dragged like a suitcase behind him."

I am not the only one who has complained to Layton about the number of throw-away poems he has published, which seem to draw energy and attention from his best work. His response has been one of amused tolerance, insisting that it is the task of history and the critic to sort out the wheat from the chaff. The poet's task is to write, not fearful of doing something to offend the puritans, the academics, and the dullards. Even the weakest poems, he seems to say, clear the ground or prepare the way for the best.

It is this best work that I want to celebrate, once again, by recalling some observations that I made several years ago in *Waves* magazine, where I focused on a single line of Layton's poetry:

"And the inescapable lousiness of growing old."

This line is from his unforgettable elegy on the death of this mother, called "Keine Lazarovitch," and it's one that has stayed with me long after many catchier lines have been forgotten.

The imagery is not what touches me here. Layton's imagery elsewhere in the poem is concrete and specific, but in this line it's rather muted and generalized. No, I think I am held by this line of poetry because of the elements that play to the ear — that is, the music. Words, and the way they are arranged, provide the poem's music. Here the words are mostly ordinary, except for the word *lousiness*, which is more than ordinary; it is colloquial in the extreme and quite remarkable for being found in the good society of an elegy. In fact, *lousiness* is one of those words that pushes your mouth around when you say it, producing an effect of synaesthesia, as if the open mouth required to say it were an expression of the repugnance carried by the word itself. I don't know any other poet who could make this word work so well in a poem as Layton does here, taking chances with a literal meaning that he clearly does not want cluttering the map at this point. And yet, it would not have been enough to have written only of "the lousiness of growing old."

What lifts this line out of the realm of the ordinary is the brilliant juxtaposition of the colloquial *lousiness* with the formal, Latinate *inescapable*, a formidable word that quickly draws the slack troops around it to attention. In my *O.E.D.*, the first recorded usage of *inescapable* shows how clever and appropriate Layton's choice has been in this context; it's in a letter from Robbie Burns to Cunningham on the 10th of September, 1792: "An inescapable and inexorable hell, expanding its leviathan jaws for the last residue of mortals."

The effects gained here have nothing to do with etymology, of course, and Layton is unlikely to have been thumbing through dictionaries in search of *le mot juste*. Rather, he seems, by virtue of a trained ear and substantial linguistic resources, to have settled naturally on this word as having just the right sound and sense for his purposes. The lousiness of age is one thing: the "inescapable lousiness of growing old" is quite another. The line is now full of tension as a result of juxtaposing two quite distinct levels of diction, which we might call, simply, the high and the low. I won't go into the possible ramifications of these two levels of diction, which are at work elsewhere in the poem and may serve as verbal indicators to the turmoil, perhaps even the ambivalence, the poet feels at this death, which is, at best, a triumphant flop or an undignified victory, since I want to concentrate mainly on the sound of the words as they nest in my ear.

Some of the weight and formality of *inescapable* comes from its having five syllables, in a line of words having one, two and three syllables. Drop that word and you have a dull iambic tetrameter line; keep it and you have a subtle pentameter line consisting of three variable feet (an anapest, an iambic, another anapest, and two unstressed syllables) before the caesura that follows *lousiness*, and two iambic feet in the second half of the line. As you can hear, the pleasing effect of this line is achieved in part by what Philip Larkin, in another context, describes as "playing off the natural rhythms and word-order of speech against the artificialities of rhyme and metre." When we read the line and feel its power, we are not counting syllables any more than Elizabeth Barrett Browning was counting the ways of making poetic love to Robert Browning. We are simply letting it happen, letting the waves of surface sound move across the organ-base; but as we read our pleasure comes also from a semi-conscious element of recognition and surprise at the way the stresses fall and the way the sounds themselves build up, incrementally, in our oyster-shell ears.

I don't know how to describe what the sounds do as they imbed themselves in my ear and in my mind, but I do know that the alliterative effect of the four words beginning with open vowels and the long a, o, and ou sounds, which impede the movement of the line and yaw like the grave itself, all work to make the line memorable. Somehow too, the combination of consonants has just enough grit and substance to hold these vowel sounds together. The alliterative elements are well spaced, rather than bunched up and obvious; and there is, in this cluster of sounds, enough density to satisfy my own very physical response to language.

Talent capable of this kind of texture, density, allusiveness, and moral sympathy does not surface often in an age or a culture, and we should not allow it to be obscured by the antics of personality. Pound's flirtation with Italian fascism is as distracting as Eliot's conservatism and Anglicanism, but their best poems seem strangely honest and free of the contamination and irritation of mere opinion.

So, too, Layton's best work reveals a strangely vulnerable and caring sensibility, troubled by his relationships with the world, especially women, but exhilarated by an enriching and life-long affair with language. And I, for one, am happy to rejoice in and celebrate that affair.

"Well, Irving, it must be obvious to you now that a poet's only good for one thing."

"Yes, of course. Inescapably."

GARY GEDDES

Cod Royal

1

You take your place at the piano,
adjust the chair, and lean
into the music. Your thin wrists poised
above the keyboard are the stately
necks of swans. I loved best

your earliest performance — how you sang
when the first wave of oxygen
broke across your scalp, flooded the lung cavities,
and drowned you into cadence.

So engine's hum is the amniotic
tide and the ticking clock
a surrogate heart.

2

Each syllable a breast to drain, each word
an island asking to explore.

Lumblums, you said, as the sirens grew faint
in the rain soaked night. Of those, you were well informed,
camping out in an oxygen tent
at the Edmonton General when the fevers wouldn't break
and tepid baths brought
no relief.

After twelve months of faulty diagnoses that left us
slumped over the catalogued symptoms
in medical dictionaries,

your tonsils and adenoids floated into history
down the storm drains
of the North Saskatchewan.

You clung to me in the doorway of the operating room, blood
from the hemorrhaging stitches bright at the corners
of your mouth, and said:

It's alright, Dod,
don't cry.

3

Though Ecclesiastes never mentioned it,
there is a time for vitamins,
the horrible D variety that backs up the drain
and makes your mouth the floor
of a gutting shed.

You place your lips around the rubbery pill
and the effort to swallow
makes your small body shudder.

4

I never knew you'd broken your collarbone
until you said, climbing stairs with me
from the basement,

   take my good hand, Dad.

For years I'd sit at the foot of your bed late at night
and listen to you breathe, inhale the newness.

Then you were in school and practising piano,
your chubby fingers nowhere near the keys
for *Traffic Cop, Swans on the River.*

5

Each year I mark your new height
in pencil in the entrance
to the laundry room
or count feet
and syllables in the dream
that is summer, my heart
crying

    adagio, adagio,

yours legs pumping, hair
thrown back, a brush-stroke of light
against the green of lawn, of
maples, higher and higher,
the relentless swing
a pendulum

or metronome.

6

On your feet again, bowing, face hidden
beneath a canopy of hair.

My heart goes out, gives back the words
you shaped when the hours were long,
the pill bitter.

You placed your red stool beside the kitchen table
and reached for the bottle of cod liver oil pills.
When I inquired of your intentions,
you lifted the plastic lid of the garbage container
under the sink and said, with the authority
of a policeman,

    no more cod royal.

7

If, on the stage you inherit, encores
are still allowed, I leave this poem as record
of my request. Know, too, that somewhere

in the audience a drowned sailor, his swamped heart
rocking in its cage of bone, sings your praise
without intermission, his lungs emptied

of all utterance.

YES, THE CHILDREN HEAR

Seymour Mayne

for Irving Layton

> So to the end. To the very threshold
> of my grave when my mouth
> wanting to scream,
> someone will say: Careful, dear,
> the children can hear.
>> from "On tiptoe, carefully . . ." by Lea Goldberg
>> (Translated by Robert Friend)

And so if they heard,
if the children heard,
it would spawn in them
those questions begetting
more questions, until they too
— with no good answers in tow —
would fall silent with fear.

Sh, sh, they will say
to themselves, parents
and grownups pretend
they can not hear, pretend
nothing presses on their tongues —
but we know, yes now
we know, whatever they say
they say, it's that selfsame
fear, and they use
it against us as they
wield it with each other.

(MAINLY) STOLEN LINES FOR A BIRTH-DAY GREETING or *DER FALL LAYTON*

Per K. Brask

Also sprach der Prophet
whatever else
never be too clever
to make a good poet
don't be a waffling prophet
instead
be as gunners in the Israeli Air Force
cowardly democracies have shown over and again
that civilization is a *pissoir* with paintings by Rubens and Picasso
on the walls: organ music by Handel and Bach

the eternal people understand
it is themselves they must trust and no one else
God being dead and their enemies not

from my heart I rooted out Jehovah
I did not turn from dragons to live with fleas

the goddess, though, beckons still
beside the unfair radiance that is her portion
all poets are magicians or murderers

had I gone out to Winnipeg
I would not have become a poet
you must understand
how all of us strive to become part of the Messiah
— even Hitler

some feared, some hated me
for I was never able to cover my nakedness
with a maple leaf

ergo, *erklärte der Prophet*
to the assembled literary parsons
and Boy Scouts
his voice reaching light-years back in time
to bounce in the immemorial halls of Horn's university
whatever else
    poetry is freedom!

THE ADOPTED 'PEER' OF YOUNG PEOPLE ANY AGE

Valerio Bruni

It's simple and difficult to recall the meetings I have had with Irving Layton. There have not been many of them, but each meeting has turned out to be a very special moment, a unique experience.

I met him the first time in Bologna, where he had been invited by Alfredo Rizzardi to give a reading of his poems. I was at the beginning of my university career and was already enthusiastic about his work. Obviously I was quite embarrassed at the idea of conversing with such an august personage, but an exchange of remarks was enough to show me that he was no 'monument' but rather a man of rare humanity and sensitivity.

I say an exchange of remarks, but it would be more accurate to speak of an exchange of glances. Irving has the power to 'photograph' you, to size you up with a look. I've had experience of this: once during one of those 'official' dinners when etiquette calls for a constant smile. I was smiling away as required although burdened by personal problems of some gravity. Irving put his hand on my shoulder and said, "Why are you so unhappy?" He had turned on his x-rays.

Another fond memory is of a morning in Urbino, where the day before he had given a lecture. We were supposed to meet at 7:30. I got to the appointed place confident that I would have to wait for him for at least a few minutes because I was used to VIPs who usually show up a half-hour late in order to feel important. I found Layton there right on time with his sailor's cap and a book with an inscription for me.

I also remember the interesting discussions I had with him about my favourite authors — Hardy, Conrad, de Maupassant — and my pleasant surprise in learning he shared my partialities.

And how could I forget the encouragement and stimulus that I have received from his signs of esteem in my regard; the true friend's words that he has spoken to me in times of distress?

The people who leave you with something are those with whom you walk some of your road and, as you go, you become aware of things that, without such companions, you would never have noticed; Irving is one of those few people. On those bits of road together I have learned many things, or to be more precise, things have surfaced in my mind that were deep inside and unable to emerge.

This is Irving's great gift: in spite of what stupid people say of him — that he is a sort of preacher — the opposite is true. He desires to teach nothing, only to grow, to change together with those who have the courage and the moral strength to do it.

I wish to conclude with the memory that is perhaps the most cherished because it involves the 'category' of people nearest to him: the young. In May 1990 I invited him to the University of Udine, where I teach, for a poetry reading and a lecture on the role of the poet in contemporary society. I won't go into a description of the success of his performance, because I would be saying the obvious; his ability to communicate, and the clear literary value of his work are well known. What I did consider remarkable was the liveliness of the debate which ensued and the interminable, moving, final applause, a tribute from my students — from young people — to a great poet, their adopted 'peer.'

INTRODUCTION TO *DANCE ON THE ROPE*: A STUDY OF IRVING LAYTON'S POETRY

Valerio Bruni

It isn't easy to give Irving Layton a precise place in Canadian Literature and, with the larger view that is indisputably required, in contemporary poetry of significant world interest.

It is easier with the 'Minor Poets,' or even with the 'Major Poets' who hold to an ideological or poetical direction in which clear points of reference can be indicated and used as comprehensive keys to interpreting their work. With Layton an exegetical approach of this sort would be misleading, or, at the very least, limiting. Firstly, because not even his most rabid detractors can honestly call him a 'Minor Poet,' and secondly, because his poetical and 'philosophical' evolution defies all efforts to categorize or define it, in that such efforts inevitably sacrifice certain fundamental aspects of his poetic personality.

It is well, however, to point out that the complexity of his poetic universe is the natural result of a vision of reality perceived in all its many facets, not the forced product of cerebral abstraction, which he categorically rejects.

Both in his ideological and existential development and in his poetical mutation Layton has always made it a point to flee from the illusory comfort of dogmatic certainties that are doomed to fossilize into some sort of fanaticism. It wasn't by chance that axiomatic certainties gave rise and pretext to the destructive fanaticisms of Naziism and Stalinism, and in contemporary society individual liberties are still subverted in the name of utilitarian 'certainties' based *a priori* on the conviction that they're on the side of what is right.

In the works of Irving Layton these themes recur and are faced head on, with clear positions and well-defined targets. Undoubtedly this kind of stance is bound to irritate those who, behind facades thoughtfully provided by society, hide their share of responsibility for a world in which violence is denounced while newer and more sophisticated arms are developed and distributed. Layton does not wish to play along with this hypocrisy and stupidity, but he doesn't stop there; he doesn't bow out with a polite refusal, but rather he expresses his disgust in no uncertain terms. So there is no cause for wonder if he has occasionally got negative reactions from those who cannot forgive him either the things he says or his complete neglect of etiquette and good manners. And thus is born — or perhaps is expressly constructed — the image of a Layton provocative at all costs, who enjoys 'playing to the grandstand.' But in this way one forgets that Layton provokes as a reaction, which as such gives no self-satisfaction, nor is it meant to be self-exalting, but rather, as he writes:

> To warn, to illuminate, to make people uncomfortable,
> To wake them up.

This would seem to me to be an obvious example of how narrow-minded 'respectability' always uses the subtle arm of misinterpretation and distortion to neutralize all threats to its 'peace and quiet.' But with Layton this operation is not so simple; first of all because he is not easily discouraged, and secondly because he is able to express his rebellion in poetical works of a high level, both in content and in form. It is not often that one finds in poetry the coexistence of so many themes that are different and yet perfectly amalgamated. Lyric and satire smoothly unite, the former losing none of its vital force, the latter losing none of its bite.

The joint presence of these two elements in Layton's career helps to bring out clearly those contrasts which the monotony of daily life tends to wear down and eliminate.

The impetus of Layton's invective against genocide and ever-presentracism has the same matrix and the same vehemence as his exaltation of the beauty of nature, of the pleasures of the senses, and of his faith in the liberating power of love. It is precisely the concept of transgression that provides a precious key to the interpretation of Layton's work. 'To transgress' is, in fact, a transitive verb that our drowsy consciences, dulled by tranquillizing habit, always associate with direct objects, like social laws or moral norms. In Layton, transgression is not directed at a moral norm but against a moralistic norm, ethically hollow, on which our society has laid its foundations, shoving aside guilt for the recent past, a past that not only cannot be cancelled but seems even to have left some surprising residues.

In an essay on Guy de Maupassant, Joseph Conrad says this about the man and writer:

> He neglects to dilute his truths with the tears of easy sweetness, and forgets to strew paper roses on the graves.

I believe that these words are perfectly suited to Irving Layton as well. He does not look away from the ugliness in the world, he gazes upon it with pitiless eyes and invites us, almost forces us, to look with him. Still, he does not stoop at disconsolate awareness, he constantly presses for freedom from the meanness of petty minds and for the recovery of that vital impulse which can be captured only, in his own words:

> For everyone with joyous upturned face.

In a world dominated by a 'respectability' as deceptive as it is established, the more clearly one speaks the more one is misunder-stood by those who construct defence mechanisms to protect their narrow microcosms. This is exactly what has happened in the case of the erotic theme in Layton's poetry. His explicit references to sexual relations have at times been interpreted as gratuitous vulgar-ity; the female figure has been seen in a subordinate sexual role, in a vision of love that would thus seem tainted with male chauvinism. But, this is another 'positive transgression' against a form of prudery that in reality is intended to safeguard a facade, and also against the new respectability of establishment feminism which, in the name of sexual equality, tends to sacrifice those liberating components of sexuality that surely cannot be discussed in terms of supremacy or submission. Yet, as Layton himself has observed:

> The competitive spirit has entered here too,

This after affirming that:

> Sex has become a source of conquest, of anxiety.

Where there is tension of this sort, based on a kind of pre-ordained challenge, very little room is left for an act of love that for Layton continues to be an act of mutual giving, exalted and sublimated in sexual pleasure, in which self-assertion and role-challenging are somewhat irrelevant. In this context, as in the wider one of inter-personal and social relationships, classifying often becomes pigeon-holing, and the dynamics of relationships turns into a clash of prejudices. Layton doesn't want to play this game, both because he sees what is grotesque in it and because he realizes that the highest price is paid by the creative imagination, a treasure that risks being dispersed in the by-ways of daily life.

Closely connected is the idea of the poet-prophet, of the 'white rat in the mines,' who is doubtless because of his perceptive and visionary faculties, but also by virtue of his courage in looking deep into reality, without hiding behind the false screens of ideologies and labels.

It is interesting to note how the coexistence of such complex, varied and problematic themes has not been expressed by Layton in a language of artifice and obscurity, as Northrop Frye has rightly observed:

> He is not an obscure poet; his meaning is always straight-forward: he has a solid structure of imagery rooted in concrete nouns and simple verbs, and he makes relatively little use of complex patterns, of the accidents of language, rhyme, alliter-ation, assonance and the like, which cannot be translated into another language except by other accidents.

But this is not surprising in an author like Layton, to whose eye 'obscurity' entails the danger of mystification, and in particular it is not surprising in a poet of the sun, a poet whose soul is intent not on sad resignation to reality but on a 'redemption' to be won day by day in an endless celebration of life.

In Layton's vast production, alongside poems like "Paraclete," "The Improved Binoculars," "Survivor" and others in which the satire against human wickedness is most acute as his sorrow is acute in contemplating the level of bestiality reached by mankind, we find others in which the more gratifying aspects of life are exalted. An illuminating example is "Early Morning In Mithymna," in which a sort of panic mysticism is mixed with a revel of the senses that warms all surrounding reality with the breath of life.

As regards the "constructive element" in Layton's work, the love poems are fundamental. Although there are many, as I have said, with explicit allusions to the sex act, gratuitous vulgarity is always absent. In fact, there can be no pornography where the act of love is celebrated as the total fusion of two beings. If our perspective is free from every kind of prejudice, then we sense that in Layton the exaltation of Eros becomes the exaltation of life in its totality, caught in the moment in which the contact between two individuals is consummated in a dimension finally free of the coercions and contradictions in which rationality struggles.

To transform sex, and love in the broader sense, into the rigorous application of an interpersonal dynamism that has been pre-constituted and agreed upon, is not a pleasant prospect for Layton, who, on the contrary, sees in interpersonal relationships the sublime manifestation of Dionysian ecstasy.

A woman's beauty, the desire to love her with tenderness and passion, the magic of a stolen moment that can contain the meaning of an entire life — these things can lighten the burden of the awareness of the world's ugliness, past and present, and of ever-reigning violence. A symbolic example of this can be found in the poem "You and the 20th Century," where in the first part the horrors of our so-called civilization are pitilessly reviewed: massacres, cruelties of every sort, and the false shelters of mental abstractions. But the poem concludes with a hymn to life, inspired by the eyes of a beloved woman, eyes that perform the miracle of restoring to the poet the innocent, serene and curious gaze of a child looking out upon the world:

> Yet, love, when I see your incredibly lovely eyes
> wise as an old woman's, bright with mischief,
> it seems I can pick up the days as calmly as a child
> picks up a forgotten toy from his littered floor.

[*This is an excerpt from a study by Professor Bruni now being prepared for publication.*]

IRVING LAYTON IN ITALY

Alfredo Rizzardi

It all happened one fine day in the mid-1970s.

He had come to Bologna to give a public reading of his poems; afterwards we had a get-together, just a few close friends, all huddled around our beloved Irving in an old inn somewhere in the winding alleys behind the campus. Food was cheap, drink went for a song, smoke hovered stubbornly in the air and words fell like hallowing tongues of fire.

Irving had just passed the cap of the sixties, happily navigating somewhere between *For My Brother Jesus* and *The Love Poems*, but honest-to-God, he looked way younger: a sturdy fellow, with his shirt collar wide open, a showy pendant shining on his chest, a wry, bewitching smile lurking on his face and a piercing glance waiting in ambush. His witty, sharp remarks often made way for impassioned agreements or flat rejections.

Those were the days when one could afford to take sides, in a world torn asunder by defiant ideologies. Throughout Europe terrorism was spreading its deadly tentacles. Marxist ideology was snowballing everywhere, setting up an ever increasing number of dictatorships. At that time the decline of the Soviet empire wasn't even in the soothsayer's crystal ball.

Irving's poetry was tied down, hand and foot, to a moral vision of politics: his heart went out to his humbler brethren and to those who spoke up against injustice and abuse. History had taught him that love and hatred were equally unfathomable. He knew human rights violations had to be denounced with a swift and mighty voice. His vision was deeply rooted in a complex and multicultural environment, all the more convincing because of the breadth of its sampling. His poetry coupled hope with vigour, passion and cheeky openness. He ran the full gamut to human feelings, from outrage to sarcasm, from tenderness to empathy, and celebrated man's perennial drama by tapping satire no less than tragedy, lending a self-mocking chant to sensuality and love. From his themes to his poetic modes, his zest and sap stemmed from a deeply rooted *belief* which, as Pound aptly put it, was the authentic poet's first and foremost drive.

Irving's chastising judgements seldom taxed his reader's patience: the truth in his statements flowed freely from his representations of objects. His use of language and rhetorical devices played a key role in attaining the desired results. Throughout his works one can detect high flung and sophisticated expressions masterfully disguised as the very utterances of spontaneity and immediacy. After all, he is the all-too-aware inheritor of the deftest technical belabouring of the twentieth century; yet he availed himself of unkempt, uninhibited language, seasoned with time's recollections, his own vagaries, and the whims of a man one felt immediately drawn to. One could not escape the charm of his all-encompassing imagination, triggering astonishment, elation, and even a dab of humour, to diffuse dramatic situations and turn them into paradoxical or grotesque ones.

How could I ever forget the summer he showed up in Urbino, so many years ago, in the Palace of Federico da Montefeltro, to read poetry to hundreds of noisy and exuberant students, not a bit inclined to trade their ebulliency and *joie de vivre* for the homilies of an elderly stranger. One sentence, one savvy image, and the poet-wizard had them all under his mighty spell. The day's lecture lasted twice as long as scheduled and yet the only interruptions were the outbursts of applause and approval.

Since then he has returned to Italy just about every year, taking part in seminars and study groups on many campuses; he frequently went on poetry-reading tours throughout the country: from Messina to Milan, from Venice to Naples, from Bologna to Rome. I now believe his penchant for Italy was due to something far more substantial than his infatuation with the landscape, the history, the women and the cuisine of Italy. It had to do with the fact that Irving found a sustaining and nurturing environment for his poetry here. He could fully rely on the impassioned response of the public, which grew larger and fonder as time went by. It should not be forgotten it was the Italians who put forward his candidacy for the Nobel Prize. At a seminar dedicated to his poetry, in Sardinia, during May 1992, he expressed his astonishment at the wave of interest raised by his poetry and its popularity in Italy.

When he made his appearance at the entrance of the University of Sassari's main auditorium, the only hall large enough to accommo-

Breakfast in Italy. Enrico Muscetra's villa near Gallipoli, 1983.
Photo by Anna Pottier.

date the impressive crowd of youngsters which had come to welcome him, he was greeted by tumultuous applause, and yes, by whistling and hollering too: the kind of reception usually reserved for rock stars. Frozen in utter astonishment, the eighty-year-old poet stood awhile motionless, visibly overwhelmed by the resounding tribute. Then, in the silence which ensued, he carried everyone far, far away, with him, into the enchanted realm of poetry.

Translated from Italian by Sergio Gilardino.

IRVING LAYTON:
TEACHER *PAR EXCELLENCE*!

Bernice Lever Farrar

"'Tell me one of your poems. Just give me a line you've written recently," barked Professor Irving Layton as he rushed across the sprawling York University campus. How could I impress this major poet?

As a mature student — even as a school teacher and mother of three — I suffered tongue paralysis. That was in September, 1970, and I was trying as a part-time student to join Irving's already full workshop. The fall sunshine seemed to burn my face as his lecture hall loomed nearer. On the back of a faded 1960s T-shirt dashing by was the slogan: "Make Love, Not War!" Eureka!

"You can't make love any more than you can make a blade of grass," I blurted out.

Irving stopped striding; he turned and looked directly into my startled eyes. He repeated my sentence slowly, even reverently.

"That's a good line, a great line. You could build a poem on a line like that. Tell me about yourself. (pause) Of course, you can join the class."

He resumed his rush across the gravel path and up the stairs to his classroom, all the while firing questions at me about what the line meant to me, what had I written before, etc. Like anyone trying to survive a verbal barrage, I was in shell shock, as too many emotions demanded attention at once: doubt, joy, fear, etc. Gasping for breath and answers, I followed him.

Yes, in two minutes, Irving — the master teacher — had hooked another minnow of a poet.

That is the essence of Irving Layton's magic as a teacher *par excellence*! Irving has a genuine interest in people — especially student poets, any creative writer. His students respond to the time and care he takes with his comments on their work. So banish the wrong media images of Irving Layton as egomaniac or any other negative label!

Irving spent one hour every three weeks with each of his students in a one-to-one discussion about the student's poetry. Very, very few professors give this much time and enthusiasm to their students. My picture files attest to many social gatherings Irving shared with us in cafes and private homes.

Irving has an open door policy that welcomes ex-students to share their poems with him. He makes a lifetime commitment to supporting his students. Each year his poetry classes were guided to creating an anthology. Ken Sherman and I edited *1-side-up* in 1971 and then in 1972, we started *Waves*. Irving has always supported *Waves* and many other publishing ventures by his students.

He knew how important it is to see your poem in print so it had a permanent audience. Over the year, Irving has written back cover blurbs for his students' books. Classmates from our class of 70/71 such as Ken Sherman, John Oughton, Brian Flack, and others who have since changed surnames, continue to write.

Irving has the magic to attract talented writers. I told him that he had a poetic magnet for the muses as we all seemed to write well in his presence for in-class exercises. Many of our published poems began in his classes. He helped us develop our own voices in comparison and contrast to his own singular and astounding voice.

His magic on stage is possibly captured in my poem, "Irving, You have Magic" which is about a capacity crowd whose emotions were orchestrated by his words.

No great teacher is all "That's-great-your're wonderful!" phrases. Irving knows instinctively when to praise, when to prod, and when to push.

He could snap a piece of paper on his desk exclaiming, "This is pablum! Bland baby food! Give me real food: chunks of meat, bone and blood, fat and gristle! Add spice and bite to your words — not just a pinch of salt! Go read — — , — — — , — — — , (whatever good or great examples that poet needed); rewrite this and come back in three weeks."

We knew his integrity would not let him praise "drivel or doggerel," so we knew we had to improve or leave. He honestly told many that they were better suited to other pursuits than to writing poetry. Irving has the ability of a caring teacher who can hug a student with acceptance as a fellow human being but still reject their work, if necessary.

Intense passion was the keystone of any Irving Layton class. In his course, Great Short Stories of the World, I remember Lauro Palomba standing and thumping one end of the seminar table and Irving, just as upright, banging and yelling back at the other end.

Sometimes I, too, was so angry after a particular lecture that I would type a three-page letter in reply to some belief or assumption of mine that Irving seemed to attack. One way or another, he had us writing every week. He gave us the appetite to fight injustices with his letters-to-the-editors as examples. He shared his courage to face wrongs and never to be silent in facing one's foes. Irving made us think: question our beliefs and biases, he did not allow us easy or superficial answers.

Irving made us all good gardeners, rooting out those stifling weeds — cliches. He shared his love of honest, fresh use of language. He challenged us to grow and develop into better poets. His enthusiasm and dedication involved us in ways only great teachers can achieve. Irving Layton is the model teacher who I am still striving to be.

BERNICE LEVER FARRAR

Irving, You Have Magic

(Burton Auditorium — 1971 — York University)

Even meteorites
lit the sky
in awe
at your cadences,
as I sat still as a sponge
soaking in your fire-water,
you old life-giver!
Tonight your magic:
    words caressed brittle hearts
    until they stirred in warmth —

    words slashed smug smiles
    until they shuddered in self-awareness —

    words wept soothing drops
    of compassion —

No! Passion, Passion,
strong and vital.

Your human heart
could not contain all that passion,
so graciously you shared it with us.

Grandfather of experience
    boy poet,
      eternal lover,
I could kiss the soles of your feet —
At least, it's a place to start.

In loving you,
  those around me
  looked lovelier.

THE HEART OF THE ONE-ARMED JUGGLER

Nancy-Gay Rotstein

Dusk had already settled into the labyrinth corridor of the Ross Building at York University that November afternoon in 1972 when, with trepidation, I made my way towards Professor Layton's office for my first meeting. Whether due to a heavy snowfall or the lateness of the hour, the hallway and the offices of the building were deserted.

In the eerie half-light, I saw a form camped out in front of, what I suspected, might be my destination.

"Is this Irving Layton's room?" this person demanded of me.

He was in his late twenties, with matted, shoulder-length hair. His face held a week's growth of beard. He wore murky pants and a plaid Viyella shirt. A soiled satchel was propped behind his head. Sitting with his back against the cement wall, his legs outstretched, he blocked the narrow passage.

"I think so," I replied and remained standing there, uneasily.

"You here for Layton?" he said minutes later.

"Yes, I have an appointment with him at five o'clock."

"Good. I've been here for three days. Wasn't sure I had the right place . . . Lost my job in Alberta. Took the money I had owing and came to see him. Hitch-hiked . . . I've brought him my poems."

Professor Layton approached, ambling jauntily and whistling a carefree tune.

"Hello, Nancy," he hailed. A wad of volumes was tucked beneath his arm.

He proceeded to his room and, unperturbed, unlocked the door, as if finding a person sprawled across the floor in front of his office was a routine occurrence.

"Are you waiting for me, sir?" he said to the stranger.

"Yes."

"Well, would you like to come in and tell me what I can do for you?"

"I have some poems I have to show you," was all that he volunteered.

This was the only information Professor Layton required.

"I have someone waiting now. When is it convenient for you to come back and we'll go over some of your poetry?" From the hall, I heard the two men arranging the mechanics of their meeting, its hour chosen to accommodate the stranger.

He did not require an explanation from the dishevelled figure before him — who he was or why he felt entitled to see him. He sensed the compelling need that had led the person to seek him. A compassionate, generous individual, Irving has always been profoundly committed to poetry and to anyone who shared a similar passion.

He did not turn this man away. Nor any of us who found our way to his doorstep. Irving collected us all and gave us sustenance.

NANCY-GAY ROTSTEIN

Greatness

for Irving Layton

Great old bear
you fooled them all,
critics, interviewers
with your hauteur
and ripe illusions.
They dare not see
the soft eye lines
the gentle open hands
and certainly not the
heart
swollen and exposed
from caring.

A GARLAND OF SHADOWS

Richard Sommer

1) Nineteen sixty-seven. For I. L.

I'd been hiding in my office from the wife
I couldn't love, a windowless retreat,
& why I don't know, just a body need
perhaps, burst out my door & there, live,

was Irving with his arms all full of books,
the hairy aura round his dark big face
backlit, so I told him of my case
& he listened, holding all those books, & looked,

& heard it all, his brawny arms around
all those books, & asked some questions, others
didn't need to ask, an older brother
already gone through it & around & round

& gently laughing, not at me, nor her,
but full of the comic pain of who we are.

2)

For some women sex is not an act
between friends; it's a hot zero of pain,
gone through under closed lids, sprawled under rain
& under night skies' blackness & it's just a fact.

A teenage girl I know was raped in a barn
by a hired hand against a dusty haystack.
Three years ago. Since then she's been racked
by a knowledge of that nothing nothing can burn

away, cuts her wrists & belly with razor
lightly enough to live, deep enough to show
her boyfriends. She doesn't know that I know.
Her wide fake smile, to me, is drawn by the closure

of her mother & father, turning away from her,
by the numbness she repeats, that now becomes her.

3) Gulf

What I don't get, she said, is how he can
pat the braids of that whitetoothed little girl
in the street he descends into the whirl of
from his armoured staff car, his gun

hanging from huge khaki belted side
within a cluster of ducking bobbing fawning
local people, parents, friends, his great yawning
moustached power radiating wide

in the grainy video we watch, when he knows,
she said, voice breaking, that she's going to be,
all her small quick sweetness, all that she
sees & feels & dreams, dead & torn & stacked with rows

of other children. That's what I don't get.
What do you mean, he said. That's war. That's it.

4)

Cries of animals bellowing out their lives
& echoing back & forth between concrete
walls of zoos, cries in terrible heat,
cries of a woman being beaten alive

into a kitchen floor, cries of men
buried by bulldozers, amputated in tents,
herded & rooting like pigs behind a fence,
punched through with hot slugs, in gutters leaking phlegm,

creaking calls of trees tilting & crashing,
cries of hungry babies left on the sand,
small cries in the buzz of flies around them drowned,
comic bubbling cries, cries of the falling.

I can't listen. Their cries can't be my cries.
What kind of song could I make of these?

5)

I didn't really know anymore if I cared
or if I did, what I cared about.
This morning Moki heard the bus & shouted
for me to run up the drive in the cold air

but my cough wouldn't let me follow her
so I called as loud as lungs would let me, wait!
She paused, divided, not wanting to be late,
not wanting to leave without the hug of father.

We met halfway. Don't worry, I said, he won't
go without you if he sees you coming.
She stretched up then from lunchbox, bookbag, warming
face in my shoulder's hollow a quick moment,

then doors swung open for her, left me at one
with my coughing, brilliant valley mist, the sun.

6)

Could you summon up the touch of my lips
in the long nights you were away from me?
My lips could, my tongue, my hands, my body
lying whole in your warm envelope

of touches, explorations all; could taste
you as you were when you were here & near
to this beating in my veins & fire
in head & groin & throat. Remember the last?

How not remember? There is no forgetting:
nights crazy with a grief I couldn't still,
couldn't share: that presence of the absent all
of you around me, your skin smell a letting

go the trance of pent tears each night:
it was true burning & a pure burning out.

7)

A roar of wishes like the wind surrounds me
& carries me tumbling down over each day
so unlike each other, nobody
looking for me knows where to find me.

Leafing through all my jumbled images,
I try to hold to one, try to make one
but I am not the words she leans upon,
I am the acid wind itself that savages

her lilacs, trees she's planted through the years,
her lupines' soft spikes, her open wild roses
all tearing, flattening, dodging my unease's
caprice & force. Then suddenly her tears

stop & still me. I see what I have done,
all because I thought myself the wind.

8)

Your hair these days is cloth lightly woven
mostly black around your face, your eyes
dancing, deflecting, reflecting light of rise
& glow of set. Your hair is a medium,

an element to swim in & rise from to air,
from kissing nape, tugging at pearl lobe,
descending to circumnavigate each globe
& lower, into the wet forest of your other

drift of coastal salt weeds streaming with
each tide tonguing each inlet & beach
along your narrow straits, up to the reach
of ocean crashing wide around megaliths

of dreams, to the temples of your seven grey hairs.
Ah, you take me in again after all these years.

9)

Late morning richness of remembering
your slim pearl length beside me breathing dawn,
your milk in my mouth, your mouth's wet searching down
my body's wakening, skin's shimmering

return to the light, return & rising arch
toward each other's need & wondering.
A red bird burns now under the rhododendron
canopy beside this sunny porch

quick in the corners of my eye & mind
& now is gone just as suddenly
as came & went this morning's symphony
of fire we find & lose, let go & find

look: the cardinal's back. We cling in passing.
Our fingers lace again in each unlacing.

10)

My lovely friend, my heart, my thirst & light,
this late night thunderstorm is rolling off
& the frogs each sing their urgencies as love
pouring into the dark indefinite:

whoever's there to hear when I try to cry out
& answers my choked desire with desire,
whoever I am, whoever you are out there,
you're in here also, nameless still & right:

not knowing what I most wanted to find,
not knowing who, now it's you I've found
beside me in the night, shimmer of the pond
under a rising moon, a falling wind.

Out there others call as we have called.
My body cups to the shape of yours & holds.

11)

Felt against my stomach the bathtub's rim,
looked down. The sister of my mother smiled
& asked if I liked what I saw. My words failed:
Guess so, was all. She was so white in the foam

I couldn't look away, pretend I wasn't
looking, didn't see the naked goddess
under my nose. My open mouth confessed
wonder a boy of four years old just doesn't

have words or thoughts for, only holds forever
after, carries high in his double heart
through years of search through all his hungry art
to answer, to honour with words her stopped ears never

will hear: sister of my mother, you gave me
joy's vision to use, gently & wisely & gravely.

12)

Love is not a thing but a dimension
that present makes all things possible,
makes living possible, makes us capable
of passing through this time/space emotion.

It isn't what we do for or with, but to
each other, chokes me up & makes me open
to death & want the seventh seal broken
open & sky to open her final blue,

to let us take one open breath of air,
just air, just stop & look at one another,
not as father mother lover sister brother
but as aspects of mind so infinitely fair

we'd love each other as we ought to love
ourselves, our self, which is all we really have.

MEETING THE SHAMAN

Doug Beardsley

He stood, half-turned in the terror of the fluorescent lights, a book open in his meatcutter's hands. It was *A Red Carpet for the Sun*. Though the lighting was poor, it was clear that something or someone had done him considerable damage. He looked like George Chuvalo after a bout, his warrior's face a pugilist's nightmare.

"Excuse me, sir," I said.

I faced the famous Layton gaze for the first time. I'd never experienced eyes like those before.

I was twenty-one, dressed in a green fedora, synthetic green overcoat, clean-shaven, awkward, pudgy, pimply, a Dunhill in my hand. I was a department store clerk at Eaton's who spent his lunch hour wandering St. Catherine Street. I must have looked like a fossil to him. I was hundred-dollar-a-week man, good money for a young kid at the turn of the 1960s. What was I doing here in Burton's Bookstore putting myself in this situation? Luckily, I didn't have time to ask. But I had screwed up my inconsiderable courage to approach him and was now not to be denied.

"Do you write?" he asked.

I was ready. "I've been writing poems since I was seventeen," I ventured.

A bad opening. His massive eyebrows shot up: "How many do you have?"

"Several dozen," I stuttered.

Those deep, fierce eyes widened. "Really?" he exclaimed incredulously, looking me up and down.

I was in for it now, I'd gone too far to turn back. "Really," I stammered.

The eyes were twinkling now, the crow's feet twitching. "I'm running an evening poetry workshop at Sir George Williams; perhaps you'd like to come along and bring some of your things."

What did I want, what did I expect, I dunno. I can only guess that I wanted to force my own hand, to have no choice in the matter. I had no choice in the matter.

"Do you read?" he asked.

"I have my own library of over 2000 books."

The eyes glowed. "What made you do a thing like that?"

"I don't know, I just started collecting about five years ago."

"That's what happened to me," he said joyously. Then he stared again at my outfit.

"Who do you read?" He waited, tense, but patient.

"Carl Sandburg, Langston Hughes, Wallace Stevens," I replied. (Well, one out of three ain't bad.)

He nodded. I nodded, as if we'd agreed on something.

"Well, well, come along to my class."

I shoved a plain piece of paper at him. He seemed to know what it was for. He wrote: "November 9, 1962. Best luck and all good wishes, Doug. Irving Layton."

We shook hands, waved goodbye, I left the bookstore. As I passed the front window I saw him staring at me through the glass. He had a curious look on his face.

Two weeks later I had decided on my approach. I'd gone over and over the plan in my head, I had the routine down pat.

I would go to Sir George after work, after supper. I would walk Ste. Catherine Street till I got to Drummond, turn right, go up to the Henry Hall Building next to the YMCA, up to the second floor, stand outside the closed classroom door — I always made certain I arrived *well* after the class had begun — and then, having convinced myself that at least I had tried in my fashion I'd leave, bowl ten games at a favourite alley on Côte-des-Neiges, then walk home and tell my parents what a wonderful time I'd had at Layton's poetry seminar and how much I'd learned. This went on for weeks.

Every Tuesday night I followed my original plan like clockwork. It was fool-proof. I couldn't succeed. The quavering centre of my shy personality was stilled, comforted.

That fatal Tuesday went according to plan. I turned on my heels at the appointed time and swung away from the classroom door when suddenly it burst open and this bull-like figure charged out into the corridor.

"You!" he cried. "I forgot a book in my office and I'm just going to get it. Go right on in. Did you bring any poems?" I held out my tiny manuscript. He ruffled through it in a second.

"You typed these yourself? And centred them on the page like this?" (I was also big on Creeley but hadn't had the guts to mention him.) "And *you* put your name and address on them?" he asked incredulously, pointing a thick finger at the top right hand corner of the page. He had more hair on his forefinger than I had anywhere on my body.

"Yes," I replied, wondering what passed for manuscripts in the workshop. I was soon to know.

The place looked like a drop-in shelter. There were ten of them to only one of me. They all slouched around a makeshift seminar table. It was the beginning of the 1960s but these people were beyond the avant-garde. I'd walked St. Catherine Street for five years and I'd never seen anything like this many rings and hoops and circles in so many different places. And so much colour. I shuddered with excitement in my matching ensemble. I was no peacock in this costumed crowd. Clearly, there were advantages to staying down-town after dark, I thought, as a slinky blonde slithered beside me, then contemptuously turned away. I could fit through her earrings, I thought (I had the libido of a lion but nothing to show for it on the outside). Slowly I felt the hostility to my formal presence growing throughout the class. Where had he found these people, how had they found him? What was *I* doing here? And how was I to win them over? Love was one way, I thought, drooling onto the blonde's dress. Was imagination another, I asked myself, clutching my waterfall-like poems?

Layton burst into my reverie, Nietzsche and Lawrence coupled under his arm. Oh, Lord, I thought, take me out of this life I'm in. Let the magic begin. . . .

IRVING LAYTON: WHO DOESN'T LOOK LIKE A POET

Jack McClelland

In a conversation with Nora Keeling, she told me that a critic in Western Canada had recently referred to her, in a review, as "Canada's best kept secret as a writer." My immediate reaction was: no one could ever make that statement about Irving Layton. I hasten to say that I am not patting my own back as his publisher of almost all of his work over a period of forty years. I'm simply emphasizing that Layton, during that period, was, and still is today, Canada's best known poet — with only one possible exception.

My introduction to Irving Layton came about in a not untypical way. At this point Irving was publishing his own books and promoting them by travelling across Canada. A letter appeared in one of the Toronto papers in which Irving deplored the state of the Canadian book publishing industry. The industry was so lacking in imagination, he said, that a poet like Irving Layton had to publish, sell, and promote his own books. It was a beautifully written letter and it made an interesting point.

I didn't do anything about it until a similar letter appeared a year later. I had our files checked. There was no record at McClelland and Stewart that we had ever received a manuscript or so much as a letter from Mr. Layton. Still, if he were that great a poet which the letters implied, it seemed a pity that he had to take so much time away from his writing in order to publish, sell, and promote.

I wrote him a pleasant letter to the effect that we had never heard from him directly, as per standard practice, but that we would be delighted to look at a manuscript when he had a new one available.

It is not untypical of Irving Layton that he just happened to have a newly completed script instantly available. He sent it to us. We bought it promptly. That was the beginning of a long and rewarding publishing association.

As I think back over those many years, a question immediately arises in my mind as to whether or not it is appropriate for me to name Layton as the greatest poet Canada has ever known. It is my opinion that he is just that, the greatest poet we have ever known.

I base that opinion on the quality of his best work; on the massive body of his work as a whole; on his almost unique ability to present a poem verbally; finally on the almost unique fact of his life as poet — that whether he's lecturing, reading, compiling books, partying, walking along the street, picnicking, making love — he is creating poems. That is not from personal experience or observation, but from the reports of his many wives, all of whom I think I have known.

Canada has long been known as 'The Poetic Land' or 'The Land of Poets.' To the best of my knowledge these descriptions of Canada stem from aboriginal days through the voyageurs and through to the present. Although I have no statistics at hand it has always been my belief, as a publisher, that more poetry is written in Canada, on a per capita basis, than anywhere else. In fact, in actual publication of poetry we stand near the top. There have been many points in my publishing career when I was tempted to say, "Please, don't send us anymore poetry." We reached a peak of about 8,000 unsolicited manuscripts a year. Of those about half would be poetry manuscripts. Those days are over. Few publishers look at unsolicited manuscripts today.

I often wonder if, as a result of that change, which has mostly taken place in the last decade, the country might be missing out on a Margaret Lawrence, an Irving Layton, a Margaret Atwood. It is depressingly difficult today for a new writer to find a publisher. However, when thinking these black thoughts, I invariably conclude that the real poets will always find a way. That is their nature.

In every respect but one, Irving is the complete poet. Exception: he doesn't look like one. Years ago we held a party in Montreal jointly promoting two authors, one being Katherine Roy, the other, Irving Layton. We called it "The Beauty and the Beast Party." Irving doesn't look like the average person's concept of a poet until you talk to him, listen to him read — the conviction, deep conviction that comes from the inner heart and soul, come through, and yes, he remains the great poet.

I mentioned early on that there is one possible exception when I refer to Irving Layton as Canada's best known poet. The exception is, of course, Leonard Cohen. Part of Leonard's recognition — in fact a great part of it — comes from his recordings and his singing. Who discovered Leonard Cohen? None other than Irving Layton. He brought him to us, encouraged him, and promoted him. Cohen, with his best poems, can match the greatest ones Irving has written. But Leonard had two careers. Each one helped the other. Layton had one career. Layton remains in my mind — and in the minds of many other people — *the* poet of Canada.

TWO IDIOSYNCRATIC MEMORIES

John Robert Colombo

I find I cherish my memories of the man and reread the poems and prose with considerable and continuing delight. So I am pleased to make a withdrawal from my bank of memories. Here are two discrete recollections which are idiosyncratic at best.

About three o'clock one afternoon, within the space of five minutes, I was introduced to two great men for the first time: Irving Layton, then a poet of distinction on the verge of fame; and Pierre Elliott Trudeau, then an intellectual gadfly not yet on the threshold of federal politics. Over the decades I have followed the careers of these two public figures with a sense of wonder and excitement. Occasionally I have found myself posing the following question: "Which man is making the greater contribution; which man, in the end, will be remembered longer?"

About nine o'clock one evening, during a wide-ranging conversation, Irving Layton made the following statement, rather in the manner of a cleric dispensing a blessing or a clerk balancing the books: "John, you were the first person to refer to me in print as 'a genius.'" I was taken aback and had to strain to recall the memory of a long-forgotten newspaper article that I had written some years earlier in defence of the man and his poetry. I needed to be reminded of it, but Irving had remembered it. I am inordinately proud of the fact that those two words gave him such pleasure!

Toronto, 31 July 1992

REMEMBRANCES

Douglas Lochhead

IRVING'S FIRST VISIT TO YORK UNIVERSITY – 1960

Anecdotes — detached incidents — what would we do without them? Fact and fiction hauled out of the torn net of memory. I was not directly involved in this one but I was close.

York University first opened its door, or doors, in the fall of 1960. In the newspapers and on radio there was a good deal of publicity about this new educational enterprise. It was to be experimental, small in size and very much devoted to the liberal arts. Murray Ross, who figures in the story, was the first president. We were located in a handsome old mansion known as Falconer Hall. Right in the heart of 1960 Toronto on Avenue Road just below Bloor. Or is it University Avenue? On the edge of the University of Toronto campus just down from the Royal Ontario Museum.

I was York's first Librarian and also an Assistant Professor of English. President Ross called me in first thing one morning. "Doug, do you know of a poet by the name of Irving Layton?" "Yes, I sure do," said I.

"Well, he showed up here last night after the place was locked. Must have been six o'clock. He wasn't drunk. But he tried the front door, then rapped on the windows. Jumping around in the shrubs, saw my light on. Wouldn't stop knocking until I went out to see who it was. He came in waving that article about us in *Weekend Magazine*. Nice fellow. Bit of a wild man. Good head of hair, as they say in Cape Breton" (Ross was from Cape Breton. Ross's Ferry).

"Said he was just off the train from Montreal. Read the article about York. Sold on the idea. Came straight from the station. Wanted to be in on the ground floor. Teach poetry. Have readings. Told me a lot about himself. Asked if we could take him on right away. Full of ideas. I will have to think about it. He's a good poet, isn't he?"

"Yes, he sure is," said I.

"Okay," said Ross. "I'll have to get back to him. Maybe we can handle him later?"

Indeed it was to be later. Irving Layton, under probably more formal circumstances, joined the faculty of York University at the main campus, Steeles and Jane, for a memorable and distinguished stay.

CHARLES OLSEN, IRVING LAYTON & OTHERS AT THE ISAACS GALLERY, YONGE STREET

In April 1960, I believe it was, the American poet Charles Olsen was in Toronto in the middle of a poetry reading tour which he described as ". . . whoring around the universities selling myself." He was not at a university this time but at Avrom Isaac's popular art gallery on Yonge Street just above Bloor, opposite Britnell's Bookshop. There was a good turnout, and Olsen, looking tired, rumpled and generally out of sorts, was nevertheless defiantly reading, almost sampling passages from the *Maximus Poems*. At some stage Irving entered from the back of the gallery along with a fellow poet from Montreal. Perhaps they were just off the train. The two late-comers searched around for seats. None were available; so they, as I remember it, leaned against the walls, one on each side of the room, like sentinels. Finally Olsen finished his reading and there were to be questions and comments. Up to a point. The only question and comment I remember came from Irving Layton or his friend.

"Do you call that poetry? That's not poetry."

Olsen glared, shrugged and gave out a groan close to a lament. He was a big man. One would have expected some kind of invitation from him to have the questioner step outside the gallery to settle the matter. But no. Olsen relit his cigar and, after applause, ambled off.

DOUGLAS LOCHHEAD

'The Swimmer' in Child's Restaurant

for Irving Layton

Irving's wild peculiar joy,
Or as Robert Lowell said it:

'Man goes creased and sometimes
finds a puzzling joy':
Irving, yours is a 'dance with desire'
as you remember those dazzling images
in Child's Restaurant.
Or was it at the corner
of Ste. Catherine and Peel
when Lightning struck?
That was another time.
Yes, it was Child's, not Bowles Lunch,
and there was a waitress,
angel with pencil and paper napkin,
startled by your joy,
your five-minute miracle poem
'The Swimmer.'

MAUD

Fred Cogswell

*For Irving Layton, who read "The Bull Calf" to me shortly
after he wrote it.*

On the farm where I grew up, my father
Worked the land with horses. Except for Maud
(Smaller in stature but with a giant will
From her Arabian sire) almost all
Of them were Clydesdales that he himself
Raised, big, bulky, and too lazy for words.

To make these work, we used loud shouts, swear-words,
And blows from the reins at times. My father
Loved their prize-configurations himself
But not their speed at plowing. Little Maud,
When hitched with one of them, would nearly haul
A plow herself, given her head. Her will

To work was everything that a will
Should be. It did not need the purr of words
Or whips but ruled her breathing life in all
Of her existence. Even my father
Marvelled at the live energy that was Maud
And I made her a model for myself.

She loved to run. She loved to pull. Her self,
Pushed to the limits by her young colt's will,
Refused to yield to an aging body. Maud
Never grew old. She'd race forwards and backwards
Across the fields with a rake when my father
Gave her a lighter implement to haul.

Unlike the Clydes who loved to stand in stall
And chomp their oats and sleep, Maud by herself
Would twitch and prance till at last my father
Would hitch her for a spin. To me the thrill
Of that speeding sleigh, much more than words,
Is the image I associate with Maud.

After the war, when I came back home, Maud
Was still on the farm, but a pensioner.
The times had certainly changed. Indeed all
The hauling now was by tractors. Men and words
And blows had no power over steel wills.
All was changed except for father and Maud.

Forty years ago, my father shot her.
He did it by himself. Now when I die all
That will be left of Maud will be these words.

FOR IRVING

Keith Garebian

Think of passion, engagement, eros, wit, and melody:
the passion of one who speaks not just of beauty
or the beauty of truth,
but of devilish amnesiacs
for whom history is smoke that never blackens their sun;
the passion of one who lives among the blind, the deaf,
    and the dumb
and voices of multitudes
the maledictions that would otherwise be silently entombed.
The engagement of one, married to a contradictory muse,
who prophesies, blesses, and curses in poetry.
Yet also:
the wit of a polyhistor
the wit of a diurnal melodist
and always with song that lingers
over berries red with some woman's lips.
He found by intensely hating, how to love,
how to build halos for the old
even when perfection of form was overthrown
how to spin green words for young lovers
and feel the sun dying on his golden back.
Erotic aubades affirming flesh and life
scooping the air in dawn's widened eye
and making the best poems with his own passion.
Defying the conquering worm here and now
with laughter of the mind, hiving ecstasies,
avowals of love and a thankfulness
flaring in the dying sun.

THE ONE-EYED MAN

Andy Wainwright

The warrior is at peace
there will be no campaign this summer

with ease
he disguises himself as a swimmer
and half-submerged
his naked body turning brown
seduces the world
(friends as well as enemies)
into forgetting his presence

men speak freely now
confident their place in history
is not his own
women dance
thinking passion with his sword
has been laid aside

meanwhile
he moves through crowds unknown
towards a final anonymity
not visible to the blind

only the elements betray him
when he emerges from the sea
the beaded water
hanging lightly from his shoulders
like a cuirass

Lesbos, Greece

ODE TO IRVING LAYTON'S POETRY

Kim Yang-Shik

Hidden behind your eyes are
leaping flames of suffering,
your words leap forth from
your deep, unfathomed heart,
in your voice loud and clear
you sing in your verse
your own natural self
impenetrable to human eyes.

In this deep winter night
your verse, with its blazing fire
with its sonorous sound
stands close, very close
to my fully naked soul
on the bed of eternity,
already colourless pale,
you shatter
the solitude of the mysterious Orient.

March 1973, Toronto

ON MEETING IRVING LAYTON IN GREECE

Theodore Sampson

The first thing that made a strong impression was the man's sheer animal vitality, underscored as it was by his mellow but sonorous voice and a quick responsiveness to whatever attracted his mind or roused his senses at any given moment. And in his case — as I was to find out in the course of my twenty-year-old friendship with Layton — the 'given moment' meant any single event or impression that moved the physical or poetic being in him: the fading beauty of a woman's face, the gnarled grandeur of a Greek landscape, a few well-read lines from Cavafy, a hearty Rabelaisian joke, or the spicy succulence of a home-made meal. I have therefore always felt that, more than any of his other qualities, it is this spontaneous responsiveness and openness to life which, being at the very core of his sensibility, constitutes his distinctive human appeal as a poet.

The first time ever I set eyes on Irving Layton — he had already made a name for himself as the passionately dedicated, intellectually ebullient and charismatic teacher — was on that cold January evening of 1954 when he walked into one of the classrooms of the old Stanley Street Annex to meet his twentieth-century American poetry class for the first lecture of the semester. What intrigued me during that first meeting were two seemingly disparate, but to my mind significantly connected, things: first, the resolute honesty and fierce outspokenness with which he lashed out at moral sham, social injustice, and what passed for literary taste in a mass society; the second, the sight of that perennially bulging bag of his to which, as the weeks went by, my young inquisitive mind attached a shamanistic power whose true meaning I was able only to divine some thirty-five years later.

As it happened, in the summer of 1973 I decided to take my family for a three-week vacation to Molivos on the island of Lesbos, and as a result, I had the good fortune to get to know Layton far more intimately as the man and poet. Immediately upon our arrival on the island, I was told by one of the local literati in conspiratorial *sotto voce*, that there was a group of Canadian writers in Molivos, one of who was reputed to be "Canada's greatest living poet." Needless to say, it didn't take me very long to find out that the poet in question was none other than the fiery rebel-teacher of the old Stanley Street Annex days, whose forensic and beautifully cadenced reading of E.A. Robinson's "Luke Havergal" had once moved me immeasurably. Given, however, the fact that Layton's popularity as poet and public figure was then at its peak, in seeking him out I felt I had to be extremely cautious and reserved, not knowing exactly what his attitude would be in going through the routine of meeting just another Canadian (most likely from 'grey' Toronto). My fears were nevertheless instantly dispelled by what turned out to be a jovial and physically robust man full of high animal spirits, whose cordiality and general bonhomie put me at ease within minutes of speaking to one another. As he was to confess to me a few days later over a morning coffee, what had made him open up to me so readily was not the mere fact that I was from Montreal, but rather the startling coincidence that the city's Atwater-to-St.Denis and Mount Royal-to-St.Antoine inner perimeter once described a common geographical and social terrain wherein we had spent our respective youths.

Be that as it may, the ensuing three weeks of my stay in Molivos were to be a truly memorable period of intense intellectual effervescence, mainly on account of my long and involved conversations with Layton: always two-fisted, thrusting, teasing, provocative, but invariably exhilarating and mind-lifting. As a rule, our verbal bouts took place during our biweekly walks — with Aviva, young David, and my own family in tow — to Eftalou, our favourite beach which was a good hour's walking distance from Molivos. As I clearly remember, our peripatetic confabulations were vintage Laytoniana: a richly concocted potpourri of controversial topics that ranged form Nietzsche, Lawrence, Jesus Christ, Canlit, open marriage, the mystique of money (as death-wish), to the nature of the female psyche (which we agreed was intractable).

But there is something else, equally significant, that I also remember from those long walks under a scorching Greek midsummer sun. The way to Eftalou is along a narrow, dusty country road that meanders through endless groves of olive trees in whose silvery-green foliage, in summertime, sun-crazed cicadas belt out their monotonous song with manic insistence. Sun-weary and talked-out as we would all be at the end of a long day at the beach, the adults would be more subdued and meditative during the walk back to town. It was on such occasions that I would often espy Layton, his face transfixed with ecstasy, to suddenly stop in his tracks in order to see or hear something in the surrounding landscape, which was lost on the rest of us. It was only many years later, after I had read over his *Seventy-five Greek Poems* several times, that the true meaning of those periodic divinations finally dawned on me. It was at such moments that Layton the poet, his acuity of perception under siege and fully responsive to the dazzling scapes of rock, sun and sea, would be working in his mind those miracles of image, word and sound that would later be crystallized into some of his most acclaimed Greek poems: "Leavetaking," "Proteus and Nymph," "Greek Light," and "Early Morning in Mithymna," among others. All I can say now, twenty years after the fact, is how privileged I feel to have been a living witness to these miraculous moments of poetic conception.

And yes, about that brown bag of his. It was in 1989, a few weeks before Christmas, and I was in Montreal for a short visit. It had been snowing furiously all day and in early evening I had set out for a long walk to the centre of town. Upon reaching the Ritz Carlton, on impulse I turned south on Drummond whereupon my attention was immediately drawn to the ample contour of a man clad in full-length overcoat, woollen scarf and toque. Even though it was windy at the time and his figure was just about blanketed by snow, he seemed stubbornly impervious to the fury of the elements. It was Irving. Now close to his eightieth year and caught in a storm, he was trudging homeward through snow-clogged streets, at the end of yet another poetry workshop at Concordia. The sight overwhelmed me to such a degree, I felt the urgent need to conjure up the one single archetypical image that could encompass, to my own mind, the magnitude of that scene: Oedipus Rex at Colonus? Tiresias? Prometheus Unbound? The Wandering Scholar or, even better, the Wandering Jew in search of His Tribe? And then I noticed that the man was gripping a bag — that mythical bag he had been toting about all of his life. Then, in a flash, I divined its true meaning: for me, at that very moment, this man's satchel became emblematic of his many tumultuous lives as son, brother, father, rebel, teacher, poet and public figure. Thus, to my eyes now, that bag contained the colourful drama — the dreams, passions, adventures, disappointments and triumphs — of a long and richly rewarding life. At that luminous moment it contained the distinctive genius and essence of Irving Layton.

Irving Layton and Leonard Cohen, Hydra, Greece, 1968.

BOURBON AND MAMALIGA*

Nicholas Catanoy

It was snowing hard that afternoon I went to meet Irving Layton at the Tokay Restaurant in Montreal.

A cold Sunday. It was windy. There was leftover snow on the sidewalk and promise of more in the air. Smutty icicles hung from eaves. It was the first week in December, 1966.

Layton was wearing a light brown jacket with lapels like butterfly wings.

"Do you like *mămăligă* ?"

Those were, I think, the first words Layton addressed to me. Then his eyes blinked and a swift chuckle filled the moment's silence before I said whatever I said.

Mămăligă was the only Romanian word he knew. I confess I half expected to meet a Moldavian peasant speaking English. But instead he was one of the most Canadian citizens I have ever met. I could hardly believe my eyes.

His light baritone, with its urban accent, had an expressive range of inflections. He smiled easily and had a quick harmonic wit.

"Tell me, are there any grand poets in Romanian? I mean *grand* poets . . . of the stature of Eminescu?"

Arghezi was alive in Bucharest. Weakly I suggested Arghezi.

"Well, I don't know him. I'm sorry."

He was strangely embarrassed. And I fairly rattled myself.

At the time of our encounter Layton was busy with several projects. Besides lecturing at Sir George Williams University. He was enthralled by Canada, yet disappointed by Canadians. His career as poet, Marxist, rebel, and fighter for social justice has startled, entertained and sometimes alarmed Canadians. But attempts to dismiss him have failed.

I began to realize that I was entering a new world. His voice alternated between staccato outbursts and slushy whispers. As I kept listening to him, I realized what miraculous things they all were — words, phrases, parentheses and antiparentheses, digressions and intimations. That was Layton in his most Laytonesque mood. Then he had a second thought.

"Nicholas, you should compile an anthology of Romanian poetry."

"Why not," said I.

After this he felt better. He sipped his bourbon and grinned benevolently. I felt enchanted and intimidated. It was a cheerful place, a lazy atmosphere.

Layton's voice grew very warm. We talked about far places, religion, politics, and of course about Dracula, images, sensations; philosophic reflections and startling analogies were telescoped one over the other.

By the time I had five bourbons I was thoroughly drunk. The conversation was beginning to taste like a dish of *mămăligă*. Layton looked desperate. I need hardly say how I felt.

The last I saw of Layton he was hailing a cab. The driver had a long wrinkled neck with a bobbing Adam's apple the size of a *Mămăligă* goitre. He lit a big Havana cigar with movie-gangster showmanship, constructed an impeccable smoke ring, and asked:

"Your address, sir?"

"*Mămăligă*," I said.

My last memory was the daffodil flower tattooed on the driver's wrist . . .

Twenty-five years have passed.

I still remember that windy day in December, the bourbon orgy, and the *mămăligă* atmosphere. The anthology, *Modern Romanian Poetry*, finally appeared in an elegant fashion ten years later. And you, Irving, you are now the most celebrated octogenarian poet. Well, with a glass in my hand, let me congratulate you.

Cheers!

---

* *Mămăligă is Romanian polenta, a pudding made from maize.*

ADJUSTING THE SIGHTS:
GNAROWSKI'S *BINOCULARS*

Wynne Francis

In his Afterword to the reprint[1] of Irving Layton's *The Improved Binoculars*, Michael Gnarowski states:

> The conventional wisdom of Canadian literary history has had it for some time that the appearance of THE IMPROVED BINOCULARS under an American imprint and with the impressive advantage of William Carlos Williams endorsement is to be seen as an event of major consequence for Canadian poetry at the mid-century mark. (124)

I do not know what is implied by 'conventional wisdom' in this context, but I get the impression that Professor Gnarowski would like to dissociate himself from it. Indeed, considering his wording of the fruit of that wisdom, he would be well-advised to do so. Personally, I know of no reputable historians who subscribe to the view he expresses here. What several of them do agree upon is that the public uproar sparked by the eleventh-hour defection of Ryerson Press[2] *led to* "an event of major consequence" for the recognition and publication of Canadian poetry *in this country*. It was not the fact that *The Improved Binoculars* had been published by an American press that provoked Jack McClelland's response to Layton in January 1957; it was Layton's much publicized rage against established Canadian publishers for their timidity and their Puritanism.[3] Gnarowski dismisses the early encounter between McClelland and Layton in one telescopic sentence:

> Buoyed by the sense that he was becoming something of a celebrity, Layton cast about for an alternative to Ryerson Press and approached Jack McClelland in the hope that the latter would make *The Improved Binoculars* part of McClelland and Stewart's Indian File Series only to be turned down by the very

McCLELLAND and STEWART
LIMITED
25 HOLLINGER ROAD • TORONTO 16, CANADA
PUBLISHERS

January 17, 1957.

Mr. Irving Layton,
8035 Kildare Ave.,
COTE ST. LUC,
Quebec.

Dear Mr. Layton:

Had your outburst in the Globe and Mail appeared at any other time but on a
Monday morning I should have been inclined to forgive you. Surely even publishers deserve peace on a Monday morning.

Curiosity prompts me to write. If the purpose of your interview was to sell
more poetry in Canada - and more Irving Layton - by sparking a controversy
then more power to you. I am all for it and would have been glad to issue a
sharp rejoinder to the Canadian press. I also considered the possibility that
you were serious and this is what has aroused my curiosity.

Your remarks were critical of "Canadian publishers". To the public this probably means a wealthy, influential and rather sinister clique of individuals who
overcharge for books, give bad service and gag Canadian authors at every turn,
but when you spoke of Canadian Publishers you were referring only to publishers
of poetry. For practical purposes this would seem to mean Ryerson, Macmillan,
The First Statement Press and McClelland and Stewart.

The attack obviously is not confined to the Ryerson Press. You criticized them
and tossed them a bone at the same time. I think they deserve a very meaty bone
but they certainly don't deserve the criticism because the day the United Church
Publishing House starts handling poetry that even a minority might censor that
will be the day they stop publishing poetry entirely and thats something that
shouldn't happen. Now I presume you weren't criticizing The First Statement
Press so it must be Macmillan or ourselves. To the best of my knowledge they
have done little poetry apart from Pratt in the last decade (until recently) so
I doubt if they've been imposing the censorship you refer to.

continued

CABLE ADDRESS "EMANDESS"

Letter to Irving Layton from Jack McClelland, 17 January 1957.
Irving Layton Collection, Concordia University.

McCLELLAND and STEWART
LIMITED
25 HOLLINGER ROAD · TORONTO 16, CANADA
PUBLISHERS

Mr. Irving Layton   - 2 -   January 17, 1957

That leaves us and although we are guilty of all sorts of sins around this place, to the best of my knowledge one of them isn't censorship. If you were serious I'd really like to hear about it, if you weren't I hope it sells a lot of copies of THE IMPROVED BINOCULARS. It sounds, by the way, like a book that we would have enjoyed publishing. I am sorry that we didn't have a look at it.

Yours sincerely,

J. G. McCLELLAND

JGM/vm

CABLE ADDRESS "EMANDESS"

same people who, two years later, would be instrumental in launching and promoting him on his spectacular career in Canadian poetry. (131)

To say the least, this summary garbles the facts. Layton's recoil from the idea of publication in the Indian File Series is on record.[4] As for the nature of Layton's first direct encounter with Jack McClelland, historical accuracy is best served by reading Jack McClelland's initial letter to Layton, dated 17 January 1957. Ensuing correspondence reveals Jack McClelland's growing interest in the high quality and broad appeal of Layton's work.[5] Shrewd bargaining between publisher and poet led to the publication of Layton's award-winning collected poems, *A Red Carpet for the Sun* (1959, 1960). It was this book, and this association with a *Canadian commercial* publishing house that was "of major consequence" not only for Layton's career and for McClelland and Stewart, but also for Canadian poetry in general. Jack McClelland audaciously printed 5,000 copies of *Red Carpet for the Sun*. Within a few weeks more than 2,000 copies had been sold in both paperback and cloth editions,[6] and 5,000 copies were sold within the year. Clearly, it was the combined talents of two Canadians that served to stimulate in Canadian readers this unprecedented show of interest in a Canadian poet. Since then, many fine Canadian poets have found an appreciative audience in their own country, and more than a few of those poets have been published by McClelland and Stewart. Elitists — especially those whose work (for one reason or another) is restricted to private or small press publication — may deplore the 'circus' atmosphere that sometimes characterized McClelland's promotional schemes[7]; but, if asked, few of the poets whose careers were thus furthered would find cause to regret the day Layton attacked the Canadian publishing establishment and Jack McClelland rose to meet that challenge.

This is not the only passage in the afterword that is out of focus. In this short essay about Layton's literary career in the fifties, Gnarowski reaches as far afield as Elspeth Cameron's *Irving Layton: A Portrait* (1985) to cull an opinion Dudek expressed to Cameron in 1983: "— Layton changed dramatically when he gained the attention of the American poets Williams, Creeley, Olson, and Corman."[8] To justify this apparently gratuitous interjection, Gnarowski writes, "Dudek's point is an interesting one because it raises the question of

Layton's relationship to Contact Press. . ." (127). Now that reads like a *non sequitur* to me; but clearly the subject thus introduced is dear to Gnarowski's heart. Witness his tribute to Contact Press: ". . . that key venture of inspired cooperative publishing which provided Canadian poetry with its most important impetus at a critical time in the development of a modern idiom in Canadian poetics" (127). He is so right; I can't think of anyone who would disagree with this assessment of Contact Press. And it is also well-known that Layton was one of the three poets initially engaged in that inspired venture. But Gnarowski does not pause here to consider Layton's active role in Contact Press.[9] Instead he labours to make the point that of the three Contact editors, Dudek was the one who made the first "link-up" with the American poets; and, he asserts, "No small measure of [Layton's] success was due to the relationships that grew out of [that] link-up . . ." (127). Are we to conclude from this that Layton's prodigious talent and Jack McClelland's marketing skills are negligible compared to the debt Canadian poetry owes Dudek for his having shown Layton, as long ago as 1951, the first two issues of Cid Corman's *Origin*?[10] This line of reasoning is confusing, if not confused; for Gnarowski does not relate success to the *quality* of Layton's poetry. In fact, I suspect he would like us to contrast the rarefied, ethereal rewards Layton might have enjoyed as a member of the small press elite with that crass worldly 'success' that is measured quantitatively in terms of productivity, popular acclaim, public recognition, and money.[11] Gnarowski doesn't actually say it but, reading his essay, it is hard to avoid the implication that Layton sold out, abandoned the faith, left the fold, when he opted for (gasp!) 'success.'

It is not surprising to find a lingering shade of disapproval in Gnarowski's passage on Layton's relationship to Contact Press. Gnarowski was a student and friend of Louis Dudek in the mid-1950s; and subsequently he played the role of Dudek's collaborator, co-publisher, editor, and faithful champion. In 1956 — the year Layton's *The Improved Binoculars* was published — Dudek completed (after ten years of extensive research) his doctoral dissertation, which he later published as *Literature and the Press: A History of Printing, Printed Media, and Their Relation to Literature*. Focused on the detrimental effects of commercial publication on the careers of three nineteenth century British prose writers (Dickens, Thackeray, and Carlyle) this thesis argues that "unpopular magazines," and especially little magazines and small presses, provide the surest bulwark against the "barbarous levelling down" process fostered by profit-seeking commercial publishers. (It is worth noting here that while Dudek was writing his dissertation, his most influential correspondent, from 1949 onwards, was Ezra Pound who, while he was in St. Elizabeth's Hospital for the Criminally Insane, was visited by many admiring and sympathetic young poets, Dudek among them.[12]) The final paragraph of Dudek's study rings with the same sense of prophetic urgency, high seriousness, and missionary zeal that Dudek brought to his small press initiatives: "[W]e are passing now through a time of erosion of literary values worse than any which can be recalled in western civilization . . .; and this destruction threatens, in a period of mass cultures and highly organized power, to become permanent. Whether we can stop this advance into total mass-communications society is the question for our age."[13]

Now, personal animosities aside, that is the context (it seems to me) in which Dudek's (and Gnarowski's) pained disapproval of Layton's 'success' could be understood. Layton's defection to a commercial publishing house could be viewed as an act of treachery: he had violated the principles, and repudiated the redemptive powers of small press; and he had thereby consigned himself to a dreadful fate in the iniquitous realms of a "mass-communications society."

But what remains unaccounted for in such a scenario is Dudek's attitude towards Layton's relationship with the young American poets. The high ideals of the small press community were not invented by Dudek; they were shared by serious writers throughout the Western world, and most notably in the United States. Corman, Creeley, Olson, and Jonathan Williams were just as committed as Dudek to these ideals and all of them were actively engaged in small press enterprises. All of them, too, had been influenced by Pound in person and/or by correspondence. And each, according to his own needs and perceptions, had proceeded to modify Pound's ideas, just as Dudek himself was attempting to naturalize Pound in this country. So why was Dudek so adamantly opposed to the new American poets? An why did he so deplore Layton's involvement with them?

In a tortuous paragraph (127–128), Gnarowski grapples with this problem. Having striven to award credit to Dudek for having made the initial "link-up" with the Americans, he is now faced with a paradox which he cannot (or at least does not) resolve. But perhaps that is as it should be: his essay is not about Dudek's problems but about the inception and reception of a particular book by Layton. Even so, the spirit of Dudek seems to guide Gnarowski's pen. He manages to let us know where his sympathies lie by taking every opportunity to disparage Layton's connections with "the Cormans, the Creeleys and the Olsons" (127).

Cid Corman was the first of the Americans to discover Layton in the early issues of Souster's magazine *Contact*. Souster, already in correspondence with Corman, reported to Layton ". . . he's one of your severest critics . . . and is very interested in your work . . . send him some poems. . . ." Layton did; and over the next few years, throughout a sometimes stormy correspondence, Corman became a friend while continuing to be a perceptive, rigorous critic. He also gained considerable respect for Layton's talents — enough to commend him to other Americans, including Charles Olson and Robert Creeley; enough to publish him in *Origin* 12, and to feature his work (with twenty poems, a short story, and a prose piece) in *Origin* 14; and to invite him to guest-edit the Canadian issue, *Origin* 18. In late November 1954, Souster wrote to Layton:

> Letter in from Cid in Paris giving me the good news that you're going to be featured in #14 with a big spread of poetry, plus prose. After what I thought was a rather weak #13 this will be very welcome indeed. The first time that I know of that a Canadian has crashed a first-rate American mag in quantity and quality. It would be hard to assess how much good this will do for all the rest of us, and for Canadian poetry in general.[14]

Gnarowski does not quote this passage. Instead, he chooses to quote, from a letter to Souster dated 21 March 1955, Corman's patronizing comment about the state of Canadian poetry in general, and his ambivalent assessment of Layton's potential (128).[15]

28 Mayfield Ave. / Toronto 3, Ont. / January 6, 195[3]

Dear Irv: . . . Letter from Creeley in Spain (to whom I sent a copy of *The Black Huntsmen*) praising your work very highly — good to have it from him. . .

Salud, Ray [Souster][16]

THE DIVERS PRESS, BANALBUFAR, MALLORCA, SPAIN -

February 17, 1953

Dear Mr. Layton, / Raymond Souster was kind enough to send me copies of *The Black Huntsmen* and *Canadian Poems*; and I very much liked your own work in each . . . In any case, would you have any interest in submitting material for a small volume of poems, to be issued by us here . . . Circulation would be primarily in the United States . . . I think we can do a decent job of production; all poetry is handset, and it looks very, very well . . . Please write when you have time, / Yours sincerely / Robert Creeley[17]

Thus began what proved to be a rich, warm, mutually stimulating correspondence that reached a peak of intensity in the mid-fifties and eventually spanned a period of twenty-five years.

Creeley made no secret of his admiration for Layton's poetry or of his genuine friendship with the Canadian poet. When Charles Olson offered Creeley a teaching job at Black Mountain College, and held out to him the prospect of editing a magazine to be sponsored by the College, Creeley, before accepting, urged Olson to invite Layton to lecture there for the first summer term (1954). Olson phoned Layton in Montreal on 21 September 1953 to make just such a proposal.[18] Creeley was disappointed that Layton could not come; but he had another request: would Layton agree to help him edit the proposed *Black Mountain Review*? Layton was hesitant, pleading lack of time, Canadian priorities, etc..

December 21, 1953 — Dear Irving, . . . I appreciate the limits on your time . . . But the offer is this, finally: can you see your way clear to come in on the magazine as one of four or five editors, i.e., to help direct the whole gig, plus contribute? . . . I don't want you as a 'Canadian correspondent,' etc. . . . Well, it's up to you. My own disappointment is hardly the point. I wanted you in at the very first, i.e., as soon as this chance came, but if there is simply too much, now, to do already, o.k. — but do know I asked you this way, that I wanted you to this extent. So that there will never be the least question on that. I first

Wynne Francis and Irving Layton at Wynne's house, 1984.
Photo by David O'Rourke.
Irving Layton Collection, Concordia University.

wrote to you, almost a year ago now, because, again, I liked your poetry, I *liked* it. And thought that, by god, here is a man who can make it, and who has made it . . . In any case it is you now that I want, in, on this thing. Just as it is Olson, Blackburn, and those of the others who will come . . . you can't live in Montreal forever, nor can you ask that you be read as a Canadian — or even think, at the end, that having been one was more important, or more relevant, than those people you have in fact moved, anywhere . . . All my love, Bob.[19]

When *The Black Mountain Review* was launched in the spring of 1954, the name Irving Layton was on the masthead, and it remained there until the review ceased publication in 1956.

In 1954, Creeley published Layton's *In the Midst of My Fever*, the book that turned the tide of criticism in Canada in Layton's favour. For that, and for his friendship through the years, Layton cherishes a deep gratitude to Robert Creeley.

Says Michael Gnarowski of this relationship: "Robert Creeley became Layton's faithful correspondent, arranger of books, and maker of contacts." In a footnote he elaborates: Creeley, he tells us, "engineered" the publication of Layton's *In the Midst of My Fever* (1954); and Creeley was a 'fixer' (in the best sense of the word) for Layton's international contacts" (128).[20]

Jonathan Williams, the American who published *The Improved Binoculars*, is characterized by Gnarowski as "more poet and artistic personality than publisher." This assessment is strangely at odds with that of Ted Wilentz of Corinth Books: "Even as a young man, Jonathan had an extraordinary sense for new people of consequence, an amazing foresight I've come to treasure . . . his genius for recognizing first class writing is reflected in Jargon's list. . . ."[21] By the Fall of 1956 Jargon's list included books by Creeley, Levertov, Duncan, Zukovsky, Olson — and Layton. Gnarowski describes the inception of *The Improved Binoculars* as "an idea for selected poems which Layton proposed to Jon Williams in a letter dated 1 October 1955." He neglects to say that this proposal was a late response to a previous letter from Jon Williams" dated 22 April 1955 which reads in part: "Maybe I can do another cover for you sometime — or, better, a print job, if and when anything's going. . . ." To Layton's suggestion for a Selected, Williams replied on 6 October 1955: "Having listened carefully to your proposition, I can say that I like the idea. . . I'd like to do the book very much . . . Tell me the details right away please. . ." And on 14 October 1955: "— I go for a Selected Layton." And as for a title: "I like *The Improved Binoculars*. Most of your titles have been real wows, so it would be nice to further that success . . . Could you have someone . . . take yer [sic] picture? I'd need a sharp one, with adequate contrasts, etc. but do think about it, please."[22]

The following months were fraught with financial difficulties and printing delays; but one bright spot (or "bit of drama" as Gnarowski calls it) was William Carlos Williams' enthusiastic response to the young publisher's request that he write a foreword to the book. Reporting the good news to Layton, Jonathan Williams quoted an excerpt from William Carlos Williams' letter: "I congratulate you on your awareness to the total literary scene in our blessed country and in finding yourself able and inclined to take on such a man as Layton. I predict a glowing future for him and you."[23] It was a great moment for both poet and publisher. Layton's euphoria spilled over into his return letter to Jonathan Williams (*Wild Gooseberries*, 66). The promise of financial and administrative support from Ryerson Press carried them through the summer; and finally, after a frantic last few weeks of proof-reading, corrections, shipping and mailing arrangements, and travel plans, Jonathan Williams, in high spirits, arrived in Montreal on 18 November 1956, carrying advance copies of *The Improved Binoculars*.

It is now well-known that somehow, in the rush of the last month of production, neither Layton nor his publisher had made sure that the proofs were sent to Ryerson Press. The resulting debacle dealt a shattering blow to the pride and hopes of both Layton and Jon Williams.

Layton's next move was predictable by anyone who knew him well. One of his survival strategies — the one that most confounds his detractors — is to capitalize, as swiftly as possible, on his misfortune, to 'snatch a victory from the jaws of defeat' as the saying goes. (This is also a basic tenet of his poetics.) The Ryerson defection presented him with a perfect opportunity to exercise this ability. The story of how he transformed his disappointment and frustration into a cause for celebration is now a part of the literary history of Canada.[24] And it is the main reason why *The Improved Binoculars* is available in this current reprint.

In a letter dated 22 June 1990, Layton wrote to Gnarowski: "I think the main point to be stressed is the reception the Americans gave my work in contrast to that of the carping, mean-spirited Canadians" (130). Gnarowski, grudgingly it seems, agrees. "The longer view," he tells us, "now suggests that the 'American' phase of Layton's career . . . was of major importance in establishing him as a poet of standing . . ."(130). But does he *really* agree? He says, on the previous page, "The importance of these early American contacts in the initial surge of Layton's career in the nineteen fifties cannot [sic] be underestimated. . ." I prefer to think Professor Gnarowski intended to say 'shouldn't' instead of 'cannot'; on the other hand, perhaps it was a Freudian slip, signifying that Gnarowski retains some doubts in this matter.

I wasn't able to resist adjusting the sights of Gnarowski's 'improved binoculars' to obtain what is, from my view, a sharper focus on the realities. But it is likely that neither my view nor Gnarowski's will matter much. Historians seem already to have lost sight of the subjects of our research. The recent volume (IV) of *The Literary History of Canada* (a tome of 492 pages), gives short shrift to Layton. Despite the fact that he is still alive and still writing, the main entry dealing with his poetry spans about a page (24–25). He is first mentioned in a paragraph about the 'metaphysical lyric,' where he is described as lagging behind his own contemporary establishment poets: "Layton has changed less from first poem to last than any of the others. He has continued to trumpet his own magnificence, as if to set himself off from everything else labelled Canadian poetry. Canadians, he would say, distrust achievement." This dismissal is followed by an insightful glance into Layton's talent for invective: "Layton is the Canadian proprietor of flyting." One paragraph of about half a page is devoted to this fascinating topic. Elsewhere in this massive record of twelve years (1972–84) of Canadian literature, Layton's name appears, as one of a list of authors, three more times.[25]

Now that puts *The Improved Binoculars* in a properly postmodernist perspective, doesn't it? So why all this fuss about a reprint of a book by Layton published in 1956? Well, it's interesting if you're interested in Layton, as Old Possum might have replied. Think of this as a period piece. And yes, I'm also a fan of Leonard Cohen. . . .

NOTES

1. The reprint was published by The Porcupine's Quill (Erin, Ont.: 1991), with an Afterword by Michael Gnarowski. The original edition of *The Improved Binoculars* (1956) was published in North Carolina as Number Eighteen of Jonathan Williams' Jargon Series.

2. The Ryerson Press of Toronto had agreed to act as Canadian distributor. At the last moment — while a shipment of *The Improved Binoculars* lay waiting at Canadian customs, the Ryerson board withdrew their commitment and Layton was requested to cancel the Ryerson imprint.

3. See Layton's interview with Lotta Dempsey in the *Globe & Mail*, 14 January 1957.

4. The Indian File Series was regarded by Contact Press poets as an only slightly less desperate alternative than the Ryerson Press chapbook series. Layton's recoil from the possibility of publication in the Indian File Series is recorded in his letters of that period, two of which are included in *Wild Gooseberries: The Selected Letters of Irving Layton* edited by Francis Mansbridge (Toronto: Macmillan of Canada, 1989), 81–84.

5. Jack McClelland was already familiar with Contact Press, and with Layton's work in particular. Though they had not actually met, both men had attended the Canadian Writers' Conference held at Queen's University, 28–31 July 1955. Layton's platform presence at that conference, and his outspoken criticism of the Canadian literary establishment, left a vivid (and mixed) impression on such academic critics as A.J.M. Smith, Malcolm Ross, and Desmond Pacey, and also, no doubt, on the young publisher who had recently succeeded his father as president of the already prestigious house of McClelland and Stewart Limited.

6. June Callwood, "The Lusty Laureate from the Slums, *Star Weekly Magazine* (6 February 1960): 10–12, 21.

7. Layton himself was dubious about this. Jack McClelland responded to his qualms somewhat impatiently in a letter dated 7 August 1959: "Some of our promotion thoughts on the book may strike you as hucksterish but to hell with it! We've got a lot of books to sell and I assume that you will go along with it without too much concern." Two years earlier, at the height of the Ryerson fracas, Desmond Pacey (like several others among Layton's numerous correspondents during that period) had written to warn the poet against the seductions of publicity. Layton's reply to Pacey, in a letter postmarked as early as 14 January 1957, reads in part: "Well, I'm cheesed off with the whole racket — TV shows, interviews, etc., and would like to get back to the quiet obscurity I knew in happier days . . . they're all lousy distractions from what I want to do most and can do best — viz., write poetry . . . It's goodbye to all that. The two worlds of poetry and publicity are poles apart and I'm not that foolish to think that they can be mixed together."

8. Elspeth Cameron, *Irving Layton: A Portrait* (Toronto: Stoddart, 1985), 272. A patently commercial venture written for popular consumption which should be anathema, one would think, to any high-principled avatar of small press ideals.

As a source of accurate information, the *Portrait* is about as useful as a funhouse of distorting mirrors.

Dudek's comment, as it appears in Cameron's book, is part of a longer quotation from an interview in which Dudek relates various reasons for his repudiation of Layton in the late 1950s. Dudek's revelation — a mix of the personal and the literary — is followed immediately by Cameron's paragraph of salacious detail guaranteed to rob the reader of any lingering sympathy with Layton. I hope this is not why Gnarowski went out of his way to refer us to Cameron's book. After all, as a close friend of Louis Dudek at the time, he could have provided a more immediate (and, one would hope, less offensive) version of the rift between Dudek and Layton, had he deemed it appropriate. Or, since his "Afterword" is purportedly literary and historical rather than personal and biographical, he might have quoted Frank Davey instead of Cameron, to wit: "Layton's increasing friendship with such U.S. writers as Creeley, Corman, Jonathan Williams, and William Carlos Williams (who had written a laudatory introduction to *The Improved Binoculars*) tended to alienate Dudek. To Dudek, who not only deeply distrusted Corman . . . but also generally disliked the work of *Origin* poets such as Creeley and Olson, these friendships seemed clandestine and disloyal." *Louis Dudek and Raymond Souster* (Vancouver: Douglas and McIntyre, 1980), 25.

9. Layton's role in Contact Press, though far from negligible, is not easily documented. "Conventional wisdom. . .has had it for some time" that Dudek and Souster were the initiators and mainstays of the cooperative, and that their association with Layton was 'loose.' Part of the reason for this impression is that until recently scholars have relied heavily on the correspondence between Souster (who lived in Toronto) and Dudek. Since Dudek and Layton both lived in Montreal it was natural for them to meet in person or to talk by telephone about editorial decisions and operating strategies. They did correspond during the summers when Dudek was away; and these letters do provide some evidence of the time, thought, and energy Layton had spent collaborating on matters of planning and production. The anthology, *Canadian Poems 1850–1952*, published by Contact Press in the Fall of 1952, is an example of this cooperation. Frank Davey, in his *Louis Dudek and Raymond Souster*, (Vancouver: Douglas & McIntyre, 1980) refers to this book — without mentioning Layton's part in its planning and production — as "Dudek's most obvious instrument" in a program to "revise the relative reputations of Canadian poets. . ." (22); but an excerpt from a letter revealing Layton's part in this project can be found in *Wild Gooseberries* (12). Other evidence of Layton's part in this project can be found in Dudek's letters to Layton from New York in the summer of 1952 (Irving Layton Collection, Concordia University). Further corroboration of Layton's contribution to the practical and business operations of the Press can be found in Souster's letters to Layton throughout the first half of the 1950s (Layton Collection, Concordia University). The warm and frequent exchange between Souster and Layton in these years also offers a less publicized version of the relationship between the three so-called 'Contact poets.' For an example, see Souster's letter to Layton dated 21 July 1954, in which he wrote (concerning a book under consideration for publication), ". . .

hardly up to me. The Press is really yours and Dudek's. . . ." (Ironically, a note by Mansbridge (*Wild Gooseberries*, 193) serves to perpetuate a false perception of this relationship: "Souster had been closely [? — in the mind of the public, perhaps] associated with Layton and the *First Statement* poets in the 1940s, but they had had little contact since then." Mansbridge also errs on page 15 where he refers to *Canadian Poems 1850–1952* as having been published by "Raymond Souster's Contact Press.")

10. At the time (late August, 1951) neither Layton, Souster, nor Dudek himself expressed enthusiasm for *Origin*. Later, Dudek began to resent the relationship that grew up first between Souster and Corman, and then between Corman and Layton.

11. Dudek, in "The Making of *CIV/n*" (his introductory note to Gnarowski's *Index to CIV/n*, as reprinted in *CIV/n: A Literary Magazine of the 50's*), makes the following quantitative assessment of Layton's poetic development: "Of course, it provided an outlet which led to Layton's later prolific productivity (extremely moderate until then) . . ." I can't help wondering what a phrase like "extremely moderate" means. I think Dudek's comment tells us more about his state of mind at the time than it does about Layton's career. Did Dudek really think that Layton might not have survived without *CIV/n*? (The Americans' interest in Layton neither began nor ended with the seven issues of that magazine.)

12. Louis Dudek, *Dk / Some Letters of Ezra Pound* (Montreal: DC Books, 1974).

13. Louis Dudek, *Literature and the Press: A History of Printing, Printed Media, and Their Relation to Literature* (Toronto: The Ryerson Press/Contact Press, 1960) 238.

14. Letter from Raymond Souster to Irving Layton, November 1954. Irving Layton Collection, Concordia University.

15. Corman was not at all ambivalent about Dudek's poetry. He disliked it intensely. Nor was he diplomatic: upon urging from both Souster and Layton, he once asked Dudek for some poems for *Origin* and then refused to print them. Moreover he sent the poems back to Dudek with a letter of caustic criticism. He also bluntly expressed his antipathy to Dudek's work in letters to Souster and Layton. Such tensions were exacerbated by Corman's eagerness to have a book of his poems published by Contact Press. At first, Souster strongly supported the idea and urged Layton to encourage Corman. Layton did, making rash promises to Corman that later caused him embarrassment. (See his letter to Corman 31 May 1954, in *Wild Gooseberries*, 31–32.) As one of the three editors of Contact Press, Dudek adamantly opposed the idea. His angry letter to Layton (11 August 1954) reveals much about the resentments he harboured then.

The thought that Corman might be responsible for a split between Layton and Dudek caused Souster much anguish. On the subject of a Corman book by Contact Press, Souster had written to Layton (21 July 1954):

I'd like to see Contact Press do a book of Cid's poems BUT
(a) It's hardly up to me to say anything about, the PRESS is strictly a twin baby between you and Louis.

(b) Can you make Cid's Sept 1st deadline now? If you can't get the U.S. sales you will lose money for sure. The book will hardly sell in Canada.

(c) Cid knows well enough how Louis feels about him and his poetry: he must know that this book business is putting you in the middle. Therefore if you don't bring it out *surely* he must understand why not.

(d) Has Louis any valid reasons against the book? Poetry poor in his opinion, or is it simply the same grudge they've had for years now? I hope his reasons are a little more intelligent than he gave for not liking Olson and Creeley. But then I haven't seen the mss: Cid writes good and bad poems, like all of us.

(e) Finally, if this book will break up things between you and Lou, *don't* print it.

All of the foregoing isn't much help, but it's not an easy business.

. . . . .

Write soon. Salud Ray.

No Corman book was published by Contact Press; and the only occasion on which any work by Dudek appeared in *Origin* was when Layton, as guest editor, chose to include four poems and a prose piece in #18, the issue devoted to "The New Canadian Poetry" (Winter–Spring 1956).

16. Letter from Raymond Souster to Irving Layton, 6 January 195[3]. Irving Layton Collection, Concordia University.

17. Ekbert Faas and Sabrina Reed, eds., *Irving Layton and Robert Creeley: The Complete Correspondence, 1953–1978* (Montreal, Kingston, London, Buffalo: McGill-Queen's, 1990), 3. Both Francis Mansbridge (*Wild Gooseberries*), and Elspeth Cameron in her biography, have failed to accurately record the facts of the Creeley/Layton correspondence. Mansbridge (*Wild Gooseberries*, 17) gives the wrong date (out by a year) above a letter from Layton to Creeley which Mansbridge cites as their "first extant communication." (Mansbridge was probably misled by Layton's error (one common enough) in dating his letter "January 1, 1953" instead of 1954.) And on page 47 of *Wild Gooseberries*, Mansbridge mistakenly takes Layton's reference to Creeley's "description of D —" as an allusion to Dudek. (It actually refers to Edward Dahlberg.) Cameron's treatment, in *Irving Layton: A Portrait*, of the Creeley/Layton relationship is so distorted and the facts so garbled as to defy brief clarification. One glaring example must suffice: on page 204, a chapter begins with an excerpt from a letter "Layton wrote in January 1953 to the American poet Robert Creeley." This excerpt is beyond doubt not just the most, but *only* lurid passage to be found in the twenty-five years of correspondence Layton shared with Creeley. The misrepresentation here — the passage quoted having obviously been chosen for its sensational appeal — is compounded by the fact that Cameron has misdated the letter. In "January 1953" the exchange of letters had not even begun. Creeley initiated the correspondence with a letter to Layton dated 17 February 1953. There can be no excuse for similar errors, distortions, and misrepresentations since the publication of Faas and Reed's work.

18. Tim Hunter. " 'The North American States': Charles Olson's Letters to Irving Layton," *Line*, no. 13 (Spring 1989),

19. Faas and Reed, 73–75.

20. Louis Dudek's 'fixer' (in Gnarowski's sense of the word), was Ezra Pound. It was Pound who put Dudek in touch with Cid Corman, Paul Blackburn, and other young American poets, while Dudek was living in New York; and Pound gave Dudek a list of people to visit when Dudek went to Europe for his summer holidays in 1953. It seems not to have occurred to Layton to label his friend Dudek's liaison with Pound, and with Blackburn and other young poets in New York as "clandestine and disloyal," even though Corman wrote slyly to Layton (8 February 1954) "Don't know why the kids in New York are quite so eager to blast your work . . ."

21. Elliott Anderson and Mary Kinzie, eds. *The Little Magazine in America: A Modern Documentary History* (Yonkers, N.Y.: Pushcart Press, 1978), 599.

22. Letter from Jonathan Williams to Irving Layton. Irving Layton Collection, Concordia University.

23. By this time, the aging W.C. Williams had suffered several strokes, but he remained unfailingly generous in support of those writers whose work he enjoyed. Layton's colleagues, Souster, and Dudek, could each boast of having received encouraging words from him, but neither of them was lucky enough to have one of their books prefaced by the man Gnarowski describes as "the great eminence of modern poetry."

24. Layton is most likely to confirm his detractors' worst suspicions, and to alienate even some sympathizers, when he gloats over his triumphs, as he did in his letter to Jon Williams dated 11 January 1957 (*Wild Gooseberries*, 80–81): "Well, this may be it, this may be the long-expected break, the long gravy slide into fame and fortune . . ." The remainder of this excerpt will doubtless be seen by some as being unforgivably cynical and materialistic.

25. Dudek is given even shorter shrift. The main entry for him (115) consists of one paragraph devoted to his recent critical essays. Elsewhere, his name is listed three times among those of other writers; two of those mentions refer to his *Dk / Some Letters of Ezra Pound.*

HOMAGE TO IRVING LAYTON

Ralph Gustafson

Where I first met Irving is in the mists of time. It was not the Boer War as some recent critics imply. To be boring is not a part of Irving certainly, and he is three years younger than I am. When I met him is before I met him. Irving was in the military at Petawawa learning to shoot cannon; I was in New York with the British Information Services in 1943 when I put two of Irving's poems in the Canadian issue of *Voices* magazine in the United States. I became hooked on Layton's books of poetry before, believe it or not, anybody thither and yon knew poetry was being written by Layton. As soon as the Pelicans turned into Penguins — the logos of those anthologies of Canadian poetry that I did for Penguin Books published in England when few in Canada and no one outside of Canada thought a poem could be written by somebody born in Canada — thirty-three years ago, that first Penguin hatched five poems by Layton, and the poems hatched are as fresh as ever. In that early introduction I proclaimed that Canadian poets with angry conviction were sticking to values like love, nonconformity, and were anathematizing the stapled forms of life. Of Layton, I go on to say: "Layton identified himself with the truth that natural man is a creation of nobility." Notice that word "natural." Layton's sensuous, sexual man was being identified back in the years when Canadians were thinking man shouldn't be born that way.

But Canadian poetry was breaking through. In 1958 on a panel that A.J.M. Smith arranged at Michigan State University with Morley Callaghan, Leon Edel, Robert Weaver, and myself, about Canadian writing, I asked the American audience, "need the United States be provincial?" The following year Canadian poets were invited to read at the YMHA in New York City. Betty and I had a two-room apartment on West 168th Street and the contingent came back to our place after the reading. Frank Scott promptly fell asleep in our brown-leather easy chair; Leonard Cohen was cherubic but uninnocent; Ron Everson went around in strong suspenders; Jack McClelland, always ready to risk bankruptcy for the cause of poetry, concocted something serious with Irving (probably in his usual style, a duet on kazoos on the steps of the town hall of Toronto to promote his book — alas, commercial publishers in Toronto have now gone commercial); Jonathan Williams of North Carolina appeared (his little press published Irving's well-improved *Binoculars*). Others came. It was a tight squeeze, exemplified by Irving with a damsel in our other easy chair.

The other flashback I have of Irving giving his all, is one taken at my house in North Hatley after the reading at the Arts Festival of Bishop's University in Lennoxville. Irving is in the same easy chair, this time not with one student but two — I gather, though, that their devotion to literature was not perfect.

A few years later, at Frank's place in Montreal, after we had seen the National Film Board's film of Leonard Cohen in a bath-tub, the conversation was all literary if not entirely prohibitive. Irving is seated in front of a coffee-table with four bottles on it. Leonard came in and announced Bob Dylan to be the greatest poet in North America. Arthur Smith had said that he "wouldn't go across the street" to hear Dylan. Frank went out down the street, bought two long-playing records of Dylan, came back, and judiciously started to run them on his portable gramophone. Purdy left the room; Frank said that he had wasted ten dollars; Eldon Grier gave Irving's drink more tonic, and Doug Jones ran off the road at Waterloo (Quebec) going home.

In 1981 at the Fourth International Congress of the Italian Association for Canadian Studies in Messina, Sicily, with Scylla across the straits, Charybdis up the coast, I opened the odyssey with a reading. Irving at the Palazzo Corvaia in Taormin closed the journey with a reading. As Irving summed it up: we were a couple of bookends. No Ulysses we, trying to get to Ithaca. Irving read with verve. What impressed me was that Irving had taken to wearing a mandala, a schematised emblem of the universe.

But the warmest, most memorable emblem is one of midwinter 1963, one of Irving at our house in North Hatley, Israel Lazarovitch sitting under the coloured lights of the pagan Christmas tree, eating sugar-on-snow. What more Canadian, but universally desirable, metaphor would we want? Not war-drums beaten outside the government in Winnipeg, Irish jigs in costume on the steps of Ottawa, not WASP "gentility" and its "fights form reality" that Irving writes about, but a quality much more compatible — common, accessible humanity. That moment I have not forgotten.

To summon this humanity to our attention all of Layton's eloquence and passion has been devoted. Above all he has summoned our attention to the greatest subservience to evil that has defiled human history — the Holocaust. If one depiction of this were not so soul-shattering it would be hilarious: the picture of the little Jewish boy, his arms raised before the carbine-toting Nazi slob. The picture comes from the Yivo Institute of Jewish Research, and was reprinted in the *New York Times* on April 20, 1975. My poem "The Newspaper" is dated May 18 of that year:

> That photo of the little Jew in the cap,
> Back to the gun held by the Nazi
> with splay feet aware of the camera,
> I turn over. I don't want to see it.
> As a member of the human race. I am
> Civilized. I am happy. I flap the
> Newspaper with the picture over
> So that when it is picked up to be taken
> Down cellar to be put with the trash
> I won't see it. I am sensitive.
> The little boy is dead. He went
> Through death. The cap is his best one.
> He has brown eyes. He does not
> Understand. Putting your hands
> Up in front of the carbine prevents
> The bullet. He is with the others.
> Some of them he knows, so
> It is all right. I turn
> The paper over, the pictures face
> Down.

It is Irving who prevents that.

Many years ago, when Canadian poetry was burgeoning, I said somewhere in print that Canadian poetry had two poets who possessed "the Grand Style." Someone from Quebec City wrote me: would I please tell him who they were? I wrote back: A.M. Klein and Irving Layton. You don't have to look far to know that Layton's style

Irving Layton, Ralph Gustafson, and Al Purdy.
University of Toronto, 12 November 1987.
Photo: Betty Gustafson.

is the grand style. By that I mean grand in content, if you will, but beyond that, the roving, rhythmical syllabic music inescapable no matter what the content expressed is — trivial, tyrannical, tranquil. If the poet has not linguistic resonance appropriate to the metrical moment, he is no poet. Those thirty-three years ago with Irving eating sugar-on-snow, we talked music and poetry. I have not forgotten Irving's engagement harboured in valid modesty. Love of language! You find it everywhere in Layton's poetry brawling, reflective, or whatever. It is a unique poet who would use Ithaca and Helios as metaphor for detumescence but there it is, whether or not the grand style:

> Is Helios waiting in the blue sky for
> the zenith's inevitable hammerstroke
> timed to fall on his brass gong
> at the exact instant of plenitude and decline
>
> The total white exquisiteness before corruption
> when the wave's wide flaunting crest
> with smash and tumult prepares to break
> into bleak nothingness on Ithaca's shore
>   ("ecstasy and fate are one")

The poem has no period at its end. So, Layton's transcendence, grandeur, have no period. Here he sits, Adam in "As You Like It": "My age is lusty winter, / Frostly, but kindly."
    I have a poem in my latest book, a poem called "Irving"

> This man, grandiloquent,
> Boastful,
> Humble before goodness,
> As the tumbling night,
> The aerobatics of sun,
> Foolstruck,
> In the glory of rage,
> The astonishment of words,
> Like Joshua, commands
> Contradictions,
> That all negatives
> As those walls
> Be brought down.

THOSE GOOD OLD *FIRST STATEMENT* DAYS

Raymond Souster

for Irving Layton on your eightieth

Your nephew, Bill Goldberg,
now a radar operator
at RCAF Station, Sydney,
where I'd hung my airman's cap
since January 1942,

gave me your Montreal address
on University Street, and one sultry summer day
in '43 I stepped off the Ocean Limited
at Bonaventure Station, walked up one block
and banged on your battered front door.

It was only 7 a.m., so I'm sure
you and Betty had been sound asleep,
but eventually you came down
the narrow, rickety stairs, showed no annoyance
as you gave me an instant handshake
that almost made me wince, then took me upstairs
to your second floor studio room
where Betty made hot coffee,
even boiled an egg just for me —
it was like a homecoming.

An hour later, a thousand words later,
you both went off to work, proof-reading part-time
at the *Star*, while I curled up on the couch,
slept through until noon without any trouble.

That night the three of us dined
at a downtown cafe, where gypsy music sobbed
and the food was hotter
than I'd ever tasted in my life.
Not long after, those two newly-weds,
Audrey and John Sutherland,
and Louis Dudek, a tall thin drink of water
if ever there was one,
joined us for wine and conversation,
with Louis later giving me a friendly lecture
on how poetry should be written
in a catastrophic age.
I've forgotten his words, but never him.

After midnight Betty, you and I,
a laughing, slightly tipsy trio,
returned to clump up the protesting stairs
of your downtown love-nest,
where I took unsteady possession
of that studio couch again,
while you and Betty climbed
another flight to your bedroom.
I wonder to this day
if you two deliberately, playfully,
gave me a heart-felt demonstration
of how an old bedspring can creakingly complain
while enduring the extended fore-and-after play
of two young, roused bump-and-grind experts —
it was exhausting to say the least
for the youthful, sex-hungry airman
forced to listen on his couch right below . . .

But early next morning,
hurrying back down University Street
to catch the 8 a.m. pool train to Toronto,
I could only think the very warmest thoughts
of you, Irving, of you, Betty,
both so radiant with the love burning in your eyes!

THE OLD DAYS

Robert Creeley

I love Irving's heart, whatever provokes its thumping. People need company to stay human, and for a very dear time he was mine by almost daily letters, or so they seemed. In those days, the early 1950s, his poems were so free of conscious literary artifice or, better, they were entirely Irving's unique conversion of his reading of the great English poets, to a manner only he could make vivid, relaxed, and always, graceful. There was an aura of the so-called real world in him that I loved and respected, a tough, ebullient address, a cocky response to whoever would presume to ignore him. At a time of such flattened social and political conditions, he was singularly useful. I recall he was not permitted into the States one time because of his politics. It was always wondrous to know anyone with sufficient 'politics' to make any difference.

In some old-fashioned way we spent a lot of time plotting and devising a very different world than the one then confronting us. I would finally consider people all but dead who didn't. In any case, Irving, as an outsider, was a power indeed. He'd best know what happened when he found himself finally 'so accepted,' which the genius of his poetry did demand, no matter it wasn't his metier. No one can condemn another to a life of unremitting resistance, but Irving in that situation was immensely engaging.

A great deal of poetry involves position papers, so to speak. There is much emphasis on the critical proposal thus embodied. At times I have to think that's an active possibility, if only because I have so often used it. With Irving the poems are always the fact of whatever else he might think to say. Times I asked for some sense of a poem he might provide, his answers overwhelmed me with their curious analysis and abstraction. It was a useless distraction for us both. He was a poet primarily and always.

As with D.H. Lawrence, Patrick Kavanagh, and only a few others known to me, Irving's innate sense of balance is that of a great, sly dancer. His steps are always intriguing, always freshly specific. I think of "Mrs. Fornheim, Refugee" as one instance among many. Otherwise, because he is a poet, he sets a multiple of informations to that enduring music, which keeps one listening. I recall having just read "In Memory of Fred Smith," which he'd sent me, and writing an awkward note of condolence. Oh no, he answered, it was just practice. There's no "Fred Smith" and nobody died. And no one can play it like Irving.

ROBERT CREELEY

Irving's Poem "First Snow: Lake Achigan"

Years ago it was I remember
first reading Irving's line, "*But a Roman silence*
for a lone drummer's call . . ."

It wound on in my ear, recalling
the season's inevitable passing, the echo
of things which were gone.

The cold I loved, winter's quiet,
he made, "*Now noiseless as a transaction,*
a brown hare / Breaks from the cold

fields, bounds ahead; / Now slowly slowly
the season unwinters /
On its spool of white thread . . ."

It so balanced as sound
I could hear beyond myself
my boyhood's frozen lake,

feel despair at such loss,
the seemingly useless agony
of life's constant dying.

What's gone now
still his words continue
as December returns.

IRVING LAYTON: CANADA'S TILL EULENSPIEGEL

Elspeth Cameron

One of my favourite books as a child was *The Amazing Pranks of Master Till Eulenspiegel,* and it was the irascible Eulenspiegel who kept leaping into my mind as I prepared my biography of Irving Layton. Now, with hindsight six years later, the analogy seems even more apt.

Till Eulenspiegel was a German peasant trickster whose merry pranks inspired numerous folk tales. He has been immortalised in music by Richard Strauss in his tone poem "Till Eulenspiegel's Merry Pranks" (1894). The historical Till is said to have been born at Kneilingen, Brunswick, and to have died in 1350 at Molin, Schleswig-Holstein. In other words, he lived — if indeed there *was* a real Till — at a time when a new class of townsfolk was beginning to give itself airs, and the hit-and-run practical jokes associated with his name, whether broadly farcical or downright brutal or shockingly obscene, emphasize the revenge of the peasant upon those townsmen who snub him. Pitting native cunning against religious authorities, noblemen, tradesmen and scholars alike, Eulenspiegel exposed hypocrisy, avarice and pretension, thereby demonstrating his superiority to the narrow conventions of the day.

My own well-worn, 1948 copy of these popular tales, which have been in print, especially in Europe, since 1483, was illustrated with intriguing colour photos of free-standing, burly puppets. The chapters began with titles like these: "How Till Boasted that he Would Fly," "How Till Put his Hostess on Hot Coals," "How Till Cured a Bragging Landlord," "How Till Ate at the Gentlemen's Table" or "How Till Sold a Cat to the Furriers." So engaged was I on Till's behalf as he impishly disrupted the lives of his — to me — infuriating targets, that at the age of nine or so I printed in large red letters across a page that described the cruel treatment of Till by a miserly farmer: "I HATE THE FARMER."

There are many ways in which Irving Layton and Till Eulenspiegel are *not* analogues. Medieval Germany is neither the rural Rumania of Israel Lazarovich's birth in 1912, nor the Montreal of the twentieth century where he has spent most of his life since; nor was Eulenspiegel Jewish; nor, despite his pithy sayings, was Till a poet. Nonetheless, I'd like to make the case for Layton's playing a role not unlike Till Eulenspiegel's in the Canadian literary scene which he animated, rather than joined, in the early 1940s.

Like Till Eulenspiegel, Layton found himself at odds with a genteel community of middle-class writers in Canada. *New Provinces*, the 1936 anthology of poetry edited by A.J.M. Smith was, ironically, 'provincial.' His literary peers, like Smith and Scott, both professors, Leo Kennedy, then a graduate student; Robert Finch and E.J. Pratt, also professors, A.M. Klein, a lawyer, P.K. Page, a radio actress, then scriptwriter for the National Film Board; these were privileged people whose tastes were refined and cultivated. Despite the fact that they saw themselves as ushering modernism into Canadian letters and ushering wishy-washy colonial poetry out, as F.R. Scott's satirical poem "The Canadian Authors Meet" makes clear, their own poetry was often pallid.

Like Till Eulenspiegel, the aggressive working-class Layton played the crafty [capricious] cat amongst these preening pigeons of poetry, disrupting the newly-established — and at times condescending — literati. Having honed his considerable rhetorical talents in 'soapbox oratory' (his description of his 'hobby') on behalf of the communist cause in the 1930s, Layton burst upon the poetry scene in his first collection *Here and Now* (1945) with poetry that was and would continue to be unpredictable, intemperate, uncouth, unconventional, indecent, impolite and independent. Like Till Eulenspiegel, who even in the cradle was said to delight in confounding his mother's expectations by lying upside down with his feet on the pillow, Layton enlisted his indefatigable native wit and merry, prankish disposition to thwart and unseat a literature which was too predictable, temperate, couth, decent, polite and — in spite of claims to the contrary — dependent. He offered, indeed, forced upon us, the unnerving in place of the enervated.

Without the startling, uncivilized voice of Irving Layton, Canadian poetry might well have languished for decades longer in a quasi-colonial stupor. His penchant for unsettling the literary elite, not to mention those in authority wherever he found them, widened and broadened the possibilities of poetry, and indeed of fiction. Marion Engel once told me, for example, that it was Layton's bawdy verse that enabled her to write of menstruation. Layton shouted rudely in the hushed halls of the academe; was deliberately ill-mannered in polite society; challenged the arbiters of religious rituals; and pooh-poohed those with financial and political clout. Above all, he threw open the doors and windows and insisted that poetry take great gulps of fresh air and admit that life was at heart a matter of physical zest and metaphysical longings. In doing so he invigorated Canadian letters, called attention to what would now be called ethnicity, and accelerated our literary move to modernity to an extent that can scarcely be measured.

Unlike A.M. Klein before him, whose scholarly acumen and social status wed him to decorum; and unlike Mordecai Richler after him, whose ability to detach himself enabled him to take the long view and place an Eulenspiegel-like character in perspective, Layton *personified* the anti-social and unconventional dynamism that makes Till Eulenspiegel an engaging charmer. Layton wrote as he lived, from *inside* that dynamic, upsetting, transformative experience. He was the very incarnation of youthful energy, creative vitality and the unbridled will to revolt against all who counsel: "Settle down," "Get a job," "Be ordinary."

Like Till Eulenspiegel, Irving Layton was and has remained *extra* ordinary, a highly visible reminder in a country that tends to err on the side of caution, that to create means to destroy, and that creativity stems fundamentally from irrepressible physical and sexual exuberance, the uncontrolled urge to overthrow and reinvent the incorrigible delight in playful tricks. For this reason, Layton has always sided with the rebel angels, at times with the criminal. His powerful prefaces salute such models as Blake and Whitman, Nietzsche, Jack the Ripper.

This uncooperative attitude to life, which insists on intransigence, ultimately cooks a snoot at Death. If playing with words makes one kind of bid for immortality, pitting wit against authority makes another. The last tale in *The Amazing Pranks of Master Till Eulenspiegel* shows Till's coffin up-ended, phallic-like, after it has slipped from its ropes the wrong way into the open grave. Defiant to the end, Till will not even take death lying down. Just like Till

Eulenspiegel, Layton has long planned to outwit death. Green in his old age, he's warned us for years that as his final prank he will pole-vault right over his grave.

THE UNCANADIAN BARD OF CANADA

George Woodcock

I imagine I am far from alone in the ambivalence of my attitude to Irving Layton. I have never been among his friends or close associates; we met only once, circling each other like suspicious bears. Yet we have corresponded, and like many others I have a collection of postcards sent through the mail with strong messages for all to read. They were in some ways — and often obscenely — contemptuous rather than complimentary, though occasionally I would say or do something that would prompt Irving to say, "George, you're on the side of the angels." I never asked which angels he admired, Yahweh's or Lucifer's. I have always been on the side of the old light-bearer.

I was impressed by Layton's vanity, but even more by his loyalty. Sometime in the 1960s I wrote a long essay on him, "A Grab at Proteus," in which I took his best poetry enthusiastically as well as seriously, but also pointed at the large weight of bad, unshaped verse he allowed to remain in his *Collected Poems*. A grandly romantic imagination, I suggested, was his virtue. It had — I counted — produced thirty-five first-rate poems out of a total of 385 in the *Collected Poems*, and that was a remarkably high average for any poet, even though some of the dross was extraordinarily bad. What was striking was that he did not seem really to know good poems from bad poems.

At the same time I wrote an essay on Layton's friend, Leonard Cohen, in which I criticised Cohen for the facile ease of his eminently singable verse, his outdated decadence. What I said is beside the point in this context. What is not is Layton's reaction. He had accepted my essay on him, in spite of my often harsh criticism, as the best piece anyone had yet written about him, and complained rather quietly about the occasional remark. But the criticism of his friend Cohen, however justified, stirred him to anger, and rated at least three of his more lurid postcards.

Looking back over the past twenty years I realize that now I would probably say not a great deal more than I said in "A Grab at Proteus" in 1966. Layton had written most of the poems by which we shall remember him by the time he was fifty-five. And for those thirty or forty poems we fairly honour him as one of Canada's finest poets.

But I can hardly call Layton a "Canadian" poet — for there is nothing in his verse of the mindless nationalism that was so widespread in our literary circles during the 1950s and 1960s; for his Canada is mainly a place of puritanism and hypocrisy to be duly denounced. But he does stand, with all the superbness of his English eloquence at its best, one of the world's most notable recent romantic poets.

Layton really sees himself as a bard, for he sets high store by the vocation of poet, and this stance has amazed most of us on and off. Yet as a Welshman I value the bardic tradition, and like Shelley I see the importance of poetry as a key to the moral life, even if poets should never be so much as even "unacknowledged" legislators.

Quite apart from his quality as a poet and those three dozen great poems, I think Layton did a great service to poetry and poets in a civilized society. More than that, he took to speech as a wandering poet, and with his rough voice and prize-fighter's looks, declaimed his verse to enthusiastic thousands at universities and elsewhere. It is not my style, but I admire the zeal evoked. Layton's ego may indeed have been stimulated by such efforts, but so was the cause of poetry, as it was by similar reading tours at the time by Birney and Purdy.

We are two of an age, Layton and I, born in 1912 at opposite ends of the earth, and so I salute him as an often fine poet and a great bard, a great contemporary, without, be it said, withdrawing past criticism of his lesser work or failing to recognize our vast differences of personality.

Irving on his 71st birthday, 1983.
Photo: Sharon Katz.

CULTURAL CONTEXTS AND SELF-INVENTION: THE POETRY OF IRVING LAYTON

Mervin Butovsky

The title of this essay — which involves the reciprocal interplay of city and person, of milieu and individual poet — summarizes my concerns: how do social circumstances or historical settings help form the imaginative vision of a writer and how, in turn, does the resultant writing embody the temper and spirit of the world from which it sprang. These questions can never be resolved unequivocally for the mystery of personality and creativity both militate against dogmatism. Yet we know that in many cases such as Joyce's Dublin, Faulkner's South, or Sholom Aleichem's Kasrilevke, the particular setting is not merely geographic locale but the very source of language, value, and dramatic tension.

This engagement between the individual and social environment is sharply delineated in the career and writing of Irving Layton and by examining some of the political, social, and literary features which comprised his milieu, and the poetry with which he imaginatively contended with his surroundings, we may obtain some understanding of how the complex ties between self and world are realized, how the ethos of a community can be sounded in the voice of a single individual, how the utterances of the individual voice convey the spirit of a community.

The publication in 1945 of Irving Layton's first volume of poetry bears a cultural significance beyond its announcement of a new talent. Today we know that that unheralded beginning was only the first installment in what has become a literary career of exceptional range, consisting of over fifty-five volumes of poetry, short fiction, essays, reviews, and memoirs, establishing the author as a central figure in the national literature. Yet in 1945, when A.M. Klein, Canadian Jewry's foremost man of letters, reviewed the volume entitled *Here and Now*, he could have had no foreknowledge of that notable career. He responded to the poems with his characteristic generosity, praising them for their versatility and sense of adventure, noting that Layton was endowed with "a keen perception, a sensitive personality, an active intelligence, and a fine literary skill." But then, with a feeling of almost fatherly disappointment, he drew attention to the fact that Layton was a Jew and that it was "regrettable that this aspect of Layton's heritage is the theme only of two of the poems in this volume."

Klein's response marks a dramatic occasion in literary history because it reveals the cultural issues at stake in the raw, largely immigrant, Jewish commmunity of Montreal. For while Layton was only three years younger than Klein, the latter's education, social position, and literary prestige emphasised their differences, signifying a much wider gap between them, and both conducted themselves accordingly. For it is the generational divide that is witnessed here: Klein's regret at the paucity of Jewish experiential reference in Layton's poetry signals his ruefull awareness that his younger contemporary — like himself a child of orthodox Yiddish-speaking immigrant parents, raised in the same Montreal ghetto — was launching his career in defiance of his 'heritage,' was in fact in the process of redefining the very meaning of 'heritage' to which Klein had devoted his public life. Clearly, an alternate route to the literary vocation that Klein himself had pioneered, was about to be charted.

In certain vital respects, Layton's determination to become a poet, and the kind of poet he resolved to be, were conditioned by his relationship with his fellow-Montrealer. It was Klein who first demonstrated to the younger man that the idea of being an immigrant Jew and a Canadian poet was not an absurdity, that in the imaginative use of language the poet of ethnic background could bridge the gap between the world of traditional origins and the surrounding world of modern experience. But if Klein had heroically pioneered the way to the possibilities of a literary vocation, he had also, more darkly, shown a debilitating closure. For Layton was ever mindful of the awful silence that had overtaken his mentor, a verbal and social self-cancellation that seemed, whatever the deep underlying psychological causes, tragically bound to Klein's lifelong devotion to his cultural community which, in the end, could never accord him the kind of literary recognition he desired. Klein, who conceived himself as tribune of his people, and sought to emulate the bardic role that Bialik was playing in the Hebrew renaissance, had to conclude that while the traditional customs and rich religious lore of the immigrant Jewish society offered a powerful source for image and metaphor, it did not provide an audience capable of reading his complex modernistic poetry written in the acquired tongue. Thus, in a great autobiographical poem, he described his fate as being "not dead, but only ignored." The prolific career of Layton can be seen as a forceful assertion against that fate, a strategic recasting of the role of the poet who acknowledges his ethnic origins but consciously refuses to be constrained by a world too narrowly defined by its obedience to the past. Layton's Oedipal gesture, so brashly announced in the title of his first volume, seeks to free himself from the shadow cast by his noble predecessor and to claim for himself an unencumbered identity that would insist on the poet's universal role as redemptive agent in ethical and sensual transformation.

From his earliest poems, Layton's work has always depended on the forceful presentation of a self — in all its protean guises — as the essential vehicle for communication. Foregrounded in his poems is the perceiving mind, self-absorbed and self-observed, inviting the reader to share its perceptions only if accompanied by the often jarring presence of a seemingly undisguised speaker: the maker of the poem himself. He invites the reader into the poem's reality but only if accompanied by the guiding voice, only on the condition that the reader is willing to accept the narrator's version of things. This pervasive egotism has often appeared offensive in its self-centred gestures, or its unguarded aggression; it is so especially if we fail to recognize its aesthetic use as well as its temperamental urgency. Layton openly confesses to his self-conscious performance when he describes the range of personae revealed in his poems: "I became by turns prophet and clown."

This wilful use of the self, the reliance on autobiographical presence for poetic utterance has its antecedents — as Alan Mintz has shown in his recent study *Banished from Their Father's House: Loss of Faith and Hebrew Autobiography* — in those fictions of 19th century Hebrew writers like Feierberg, Berdichevsky, and Brenner. These novels transcribe the ordeal of personal transformation undergone by their protagonists when they foresake the ideology and practice of their religious civilization for the inviting world of emancipated Enlightenment. The encounter between the traditional Jewish world and the forces of secular modernism is one that has affected all Jewish writers and provided them with their great subject: the drama of the self as it emerges reborn from the collision between the old and the new. In this process of changing identities, the modern Jewish writer explores the often anguished attainment of selfhood amidst the desolate landscape of disbelief. And given the circumstances of modern Jewish life, that landscape has invariably been the city — beginning in Odessa, Czernovitz, Prague or Vienna and later transplanted to Brooklyn, Manhattan, Chicago, or Montreal. Among these city streets, tenements, candy stores, schools, cheders, and shuls, was shaped the elemental story of how the son or daughter abandons the narrow, parochial world of parents for the open, exhilarating domain of secular knowledge and wordly expansiveness. Or in Layton's version of his personal myth transacted on Montreal's crowded working-class streets: "I was also fashioning the long pole that would enable me to vault over that wall with the ease and joy of an Olympian."

In retrospect we can recognize that Layton is a mythographer whose vast number of poems reveal a single myth concerned with the act of self-creation. His life-long act of writing has produced no single poem more impressive than his assertive, hectoring self, a self-conscious mock-heroic figure who invented just the kind of person he had to become if he was to deliver himself from the obscurity and ineffectuality that had engulfed others around him. Layton brought to his chosen literary vocation much the same raw, dynamic energy that his peers from the first immigrant generation were to demonstrate when they elbowed their way out of Montreal's urban slums into the often inhospitable fields of law, medicine, commerce, and manufacturing.

Like all myths, Layton's is an etiological account describing the crucial transformative acts that have resulted in his own being. At an early age he rejected the identity that birth and family had given him and for many years remained uncertain about his choice of an appropriate name that would signify his fluid, evolving self. His birth name was Yisroel Pinchas Lazarovitch, but this underwent considerable change — Issie Lazarovitch, Isadore Lazarre, Irvine Lazarre, Pete Lazarovitch, Irvine Layton, Irving Peter Layton — before he was to arrive at the one most suited to his emerging sense of self. Whatever his motives, these changes indicate a desire to efface the foreign-sounding Yiddish-Slavic original and replace it with the more acceptable Anglicized version announced in his final choice. The numerous variations can be read as the most immediate token of ethnic discomfort, just as countless others of his generation had similarly accepted name-changes as the least painful way of entering a society whose social practices often penalized ethnic particularity. In Layton's case, the indeterminacy of name selection also signals a restlessness with the state of ethnic fixity and a desire to venture into new experience as a radical innocent, unencumbered by the past — into the Here and Now.

Layton was born in Romania and brought to Montreal on his first birthday in 1913. The family lived in the crowded Jewish quarter, south of Ontario Street which Layton described as "a semi-slum area inhabited by French-Canadians, Jews, and Italians who lived on de Montigny Street, a very rich and very colourful neighbourhood comprising a number of cat-houses, small grocery stores, immigrants." The ethnic and social distinctions inscribed in his immediate neighbourhood gave him an early lesson in boundaries, oppositions, and limits. Remembering later what he had unconsciously absorbed from his environment, Layton described in the foreword to *The Collected Poems of Irving Layton* (1971), how Montreal's cityscape established his own awareness of difference:

> In Montreal the dominant ethnic groups stared at one another balefully across their self-erected ghetto walls. Three solitudes. I remember the feelings of anxiety I had as a boy whenever I crossed St. Denis Street. This street marked the border between the Jewish and French-Canadian territories. East of St. Denis was hostile Indian country densely populated with church-going Mohawks somewhat older than myself waiting to ambush me . . . Bleury Street and beyond, walking westward, took me into that other ghetto, the one where the Anglo-Saxons lived in tree-lined and privileged aloofness . . . So that when I found myself in Westmount. . .I'd feel a different kind of menace. One that was internal rather than external in its thrust. I felt weak, helpless, as if all my strength was leaving me through the pores of my skin. Here I always felt myself to be a trespasser, not a warrior as I did when I crossed St. Denis Street. At any moment huge mastiffs would be loosed on me or

someone with a healthy tanned face would say to me with cold but perfect English diction: "Get away from here."

But the lesson of the streets was a generalized social version of what the young boy was already intimately acquainted with at home. In his own parents Layton had an immediate, indelible exposure to the conflict of self-enclosed personalities who, in their distinctive individuality, represented to him the irreconcilable polar extremes of temperament and sensibility. In them he first experienced the clash of opposites that was to be transmuted into the typical dialectical mode of his mature thought.

Layton's father, a bookkeeper in the old country, was unable to adjust to the new economic realities in Canada. A deeply religious man, his answer to the disappointments and frustrations of daily life was to retreat into a world of his own making, shutting out the clamorous surroundings by concentrating on the spiritual reality he found in holy writ. In the son's memory the father is more often aching absence than affirming presence. The closed door to the father's study-room which allowed the privacy and solitude for his Talmudic concentration, also shut out the actual world of striving, contest, and engagement. The father's withdrawal left the mother to cope with the family's economy and welfare. She was an energetic, vociferous woman, who supported the family by maintaining a small grocery store in the converted living-room of their flat. Unlike her husband, she was forceful, demanding, and vituperative — traits which Layton claims as her legacy to his idiosyncratic stance and bearing.

In the father's quiesence and the mother's assertiveness Layton had the basic polarities for his "family romance," his personal myth of origin. In parental conflict he located the primal antinomies that he accepted as the basis of his character and from which he derived the dialectical structure of thought and feeling that is manifest in all his writing. The terms of the configuration may vary: feeling / form; carnal / spiritual; self / world; Jew / Christian; academic / poet; critic / writer; life / death; appetite / restraint; communism / democracy; ugliness / beauty; — but regardless of specific subject, it was in the antithetical coupling of opposites that he perceived the nature of reality and the juxtaposition of contraries became his chief means for exploring its infinite variety.

Layton's attitude to his Jewish identity, and the source for his poetry of Jewish Montreal, are similarly rooted in the perceived opposition between Judaism and Jewishness, on a strict demarcation between the religious and the ethnic-cultural components that comprise Jewish life. He early rejected the religious rituals and daily practices of Judaism as too narrow and intolerant for modern usage. In his memoir *Waiting for the Messiah* (1985), he refers to the religious dimension of Judaism as a "legacy of my father's superstition and the foolish rigidities that went along with it," and claims that he had "long ago turned [his] back on the narrow, life-restricting superstitions of [his] family." Elsewhere he softens this view by enlarging on the praiseworthy, contemplative devotions of his father, and remembers with considerable emotion scenes of his mother's prayers at the Sabbath candles. But the emphatic dismissal of his father's ritual practices is a candid account by the older memoirist of his youthful views, recalling for us something of his desire to dispense with his father's archaisms in order that he might align himself with the new forces which, throughout the Jewish community, were offering the younger generation a radically altered discourse to replace the outmoded one of their ancient religion.

While most encounters between traditional Jewish communities and a modern secular society result in the attenuation of customs and beliefs, the particular form of adaptation depends, in each case, on the prevailing historical conditions. For the immigrant generation that came to maturity in the Montreal of the 1920s and 1930s, the most salient feature of their lives — aside from their consciousness of being immigrants — was the rise of totalitarian dictatorships in Europe threatening the lives of their families and compatriots, and the devastating effects of the Great Depression. The political anxiety, inescapable economic disorder, and vast social misery of that era, affected the disadvantaged Montreal immigrant community as it did all Canadians, and like many others they found some solace for their economic and social dislocation in the ideologies of radical political parties.

The radical political culture of Montreal was especially appealing to the sons and daughters of Jewish immigrant families because it had much in common with the traditional religious one they had experienced at home or in the synagogue. Impelled to disassociate themselves from the pre-modern traditions, great numbers found it relatively easy to transfer their loyalty to the broad spectrum of political organizations that had arisen to answer the critical needs of a confused and demoralized population. In the Jewish community they could choose among the Communist Party, socialist factions of all kinds, Labour Zionist movements, Trotskyite splinter groups, the Bund, anarchist cells, the full spectrum of labour unions, and many other obscure and long-forgotten segments of the radical past. Despite their doctrinal differences and the bitter internecine strife that took up most of their energies, common elements united these sectarians which, ironically, they shared with traditional Judaism. Like the ancient religion, their ideological systems were text-centred, based on a narrative version of human history that decribed the irreversible progression from slavery to freedom. In addition, their organizations' ideological coherence relied on a privileged rabbin-ate/leadership authorized to interpret the laws of history. And above all, the covenantal 'chosenness' of Israel was easily transmuted to the proletariate whose ordained role as agent for redemptive change — a kind of Messianic deliverer — would usher the oppressed into the utopian classless society. This unlikely juxtaposition of religious and atheist ideologies is perhaps summarized in George Steiner's witty aphorism: "Marxism is, in essence, Judaism grown impatient."

If these similarities in the structures of belief systems helped ease the transference of loyalties, the process was doubtless aided by the political conditions affecting Jews in Canada and, particularly, Quebec. During the 1930s the young community, the majority of whom had barely landed in Canada in their flight from Czarist anti-Semitism, watched with mounting dismay and horror the entrapment of their European families. On the streets of Montreal, meanwhile, they nervously observed the rise of indigenous xeno-phobic, fascist sentiment, openly demonstrated in public rallies and street parades, and broadly published as editorial opinion by the intellectual elite. These manifestations centred on the Jews, demand-ing a restriction to their entry as refugees and a curtailment of their economic activities. To many, it seemed that the murderous atmo-sphere of Europe had now overtaken their haven in Montreal.

Little wonder that the appeal of left-wing movements opposed to fascism and Nazism was so wide-spread among Jewish youth. Like many other self-respecting members of his generation, Layton grav-itated to the socialist groups which, in their intense polemical discussions, political meetings, and fierce debates with competing factions, became a kind of finishing school while he attended Baron Byng High School and during his college years at MacDonald College.

Both his formal education and the involvement in Marxist movements offered secular alternatives to the disparaged Judaism of his father. The grammar of political science acquired at university (he took an M.A. degree in the subject following his B.Sc. at MacDonald College) and the universalistic ethic of socialism became the surrogates for the antiquated vocabulary of tradition. Layton, whose education in the literature and religious thought of Judaism never went beyond the elementary level, found in the secular version of history and human destiny an intellectual seriousness that was absent from his experience with Judaism. And the dichotomous distinction between the two had a profound influence on his treatment of Jewish subject matter.

A reading of Layton's work reveals two distinct stages in the evolution of his attitude to the literary treatment of Jewish circumstance. In the first stage, which comprises the poetry from the 1940s to the mid-1960s, the poetry is only intermittently concerned with aspects of Jewish life, and rarely finds a vantage point for the enactment of the poem in the narrator's awareness of himself as Jew. When he does draw upon Jewish character or incident the poems are often blunt indictments against bloated materialism or moral indifference. His targets are usually middle-class suburbanites, indifferent both to Torah and poetry. So in "The Real Values" the narrator commiserates with the hapless Rabbi of such a congregation, asking:

> Rabbi, why do you move heaven and earth
> to blow breath
> into this lifeless body,
> drowned under the surfeit
> of Chinese food and pizzapie?

Then he concludes by admonishing him to,

> Save your breath, Rabbi.
> No, save your money.

And learn from your bloated flock
bored by whiskey and wifeswapping,
the burnt offerings on Sunday,
how to invest sensibly
in real estate values.

So that you can speak the truth
as I do.

The inversion of values, which sees the congregation's materialism subvert the Rabbi's vain attempt to quicken their spirits, is expended in the punning "real estate values." Here is a fair example of Layton's opinionated verse focussed on the Jewish community or its representatives. The didactic intent is expressed in the plain, prosaic language. It eschews any form of figuration, relying instead on the speaking voice of an observer who has access to a truth obviously withheld from the well-intentioned but deluded Rabbi. In terms of social criticism, the poem is caricature rather than analysis, satisfying itself in declaration without subtlety. It is the kind of poem that presents the reader with the product of the poet's thinking, rather than a transcription of process which would invite the reader's participation.

The attitude toward middle-class Jews reflected in this poem is typical of the many caustic lines Layton directed to his own people. In poems such as "The Ritual Cut," "The Human Condition," and "Stocktaking on the Day of Atonement," one has the reiterated disdain at the perceived moral failings he finds in the community that has prospered and moved from the working-class immigrant neighbourhoods to the affluent suburbs. Writing in the "Foreward" to *Europe and Other Bad News* (1981) he states that the attitude formed when he had "experienced the banalities of middle-class Judaism and gotten to know from first-hand experience its bottomless contempt for anything that doesn't contribute to personal advancement measured in terms of money and chattels. It was a spectacle to make a poet weep or explode with rage. I have done both."

But just as all of Layton's poetry can be divided between the declarative and the contemplative, so too his poetry on Jewish themes. If his social commentary on the modern Jewish condition speaks with one voice, there is at the same time another type of expression which treats of his Jewish experience in an entirely different manner. In such poems the narrator does not castigate at the sight of infraction, but draws upon the memory of his origins as a means of self-exploration. The speaking voice turns in on itself, seeking in the remembered past some touchstone to its own true nature. The self-reflective act of memory leads to insights which, ironically, go beyond egotism and self-aggrandizement.

For instance, "The Black Huntsmen" (1951) is an example of Layton's contemplative mode based on the persistence of the past. In this tender work, the residual effects of a Jewish childhood in "slum streets" intermingles with the chivalric legends made available through literature, an awakening not without its dreadful knowledge. The opening lines, "Before ever I knew men were hunting me / I knew delight" contrasts the narrator's resigned awareness of victimization with an earlier state of innocence when:

> The childish heart then
> Was ears nose eyes twice ten fingers,
> And the torpid slum street, in summer,
> A cut vein of the sun
> That shed goldmotes by the million
> Against a boy's bare toe foot ankle knee.

An innocence defined in such pure sensory delight ends abruptly with the intrusion of literary legend with its transformative power:

> I discovered Tennyson in a secondhand bookstore;
> He put his bugle for me to his bearded mouth,
> And down his acquitaine nose a diminutive King Arthur
> Rode out of our grocery shop bowing to left and to right,
> Bearing my mother's *sheitel* with him;
> And for a whole week after that
> I called my cat Launcelot.

For the young boy who inhabits the grocery shop in the slum streets dreaming of former glories, his mother's wig can be the talismanic grail. The first word of the final stanza returns us to the present, but childhood imaginings have left their imprint, taking him beyond the innocent forms of sensory knowledge into the threatening realms of stalking quester and prey:

> Now I look out for the evil retinue
> Making their sortie out of a forest of gold;
> Afterwards their dames shall weave my *tzitzith*
> Into a tapestry,
> Though for myself I had preferred
> A death by water or sky.

The specificity of reference to his Jewish talisman (*tzitzith* are the fringes worn on ritual garments or prayer-shawls) underscores his awareness of difference, an awareness that includes the fact that he and his story will be altered by the pursuer's women when they weave their version into tapestry's narration. That narrational objectification is a form of death because it denies the subject his own voice to relate his own story. His preference would be dissolution into the natural elements of water and sky, a return to those same elements that had circumscribed and enthralled his childhood — flesh, limbs, and sun.

Taken together, the poems that render Jewish experience, whether written in a spirit of antagonism or empathy, are, as Klein had earlier predicted, less frequent in the first twenty years of his publishing history than his other topical or philosophic concerns. The same can be noted in his critical or social commentary. In a period which comprised the two major events in modern Jewish history — the Holocaust and the establishment of a sovereign Jewish state — Layton's voice is seldom raised, his attention was elsewhere, devoted to the subjects which preoccupied him in the first stage of his career: the studies in the dialectical nature of reality; the reformation of the Canadian literary identity; and the demand for an open acceptance of our sensual natures. These preoccupations, the concerns of his poetry between the end of World War II and the mid-1960s show the avowed tendency toward the universalization of culture and values. And despite the fact that Layton retained close ties with Jewish communal institutions such as Herzliah High School and the Jewish Public Library, his poetic reflections on Jewish experience were refracted through his general philosophic and social concerns, or else, more commonly, relegated to light satiric verse which held the crass vulgarities of middle-class suburbanites up to ridicule.

But since 1967 a significant change can be noted in his relationship to Jews and Judaism, signalling an open identification with Jewish national circumstance: politically, in support of beleaguered Israel, and morally, in his condemnation of Christianity as the fomentor of the anti-Semitism which culminated in the Holocaust. In his characteristically resolute fashion, Layton reacted dramatically to Israel's threatened position in the days leading up to the Six-Day War. Struck by the indifference of the great powers before the loudly-trumpeted invasion plans by Israel's surrounding enemies, he saw the imminent destruction of the Jewish state as a continuation of the genocidal sentiments of Christian Europe. Little wonder then that with the unexpected victory came an outpouring of pride in the Israeli military power which had assured the State's existence against overwhelming odds. In fact, Layton perceived the military victory of the modern Israeli as a kind of redress for the powerlessness of the historic Jew. In his "For My Two Sons, Max and David" he juxtaposes a lengthy catalogue description of Jewish victimization, beginning with:

> The wandering Jew: the suffering Jew
> The despoiled Jew: the beaten Jew
> The Jew to burn: the Jew to gas
> The Jew to humiliate . . . .

He continues with a list of prosaic sentences each beginning emphatically with "The Jew" and then specifying a trait which brought down the Christian depredations aroused by the Jew's scapegoat role. These include:

> The Jew whose helplessness stirs the heart and conscience
> of the Christian like the beggars outside his churches

> The Jew who can justifiably be murdered because he is rich

> The Jew who can justifiably be murdered because he is poor

until the final three lines of the poem charges his sons to alter their Jewish fate by replacing powerlessness with power:

> Be none of these my sons
> My sons be none of these
> Be gunners in the Israeli Air Force

The very bluntness of the final assertion makes its own claim for a reversal of the traditional role of the Jew which exposed a defenceless people to continuous depredations. In a world chagrined to murderous rage by the Jew's spiritual endowments, it is prudent to rely on force, and break, once and for all, the mold of pariah/ scapegoat, exchanging cringing weakness for virile sovereignty.

If the sight of an Israel willing to take upon itself the full responsibility for its own survival (what the theologian Emil Fackenheim calls the Jewish return to history) induces in Layton a sense of national pride, and gives rise to these and other such poems which celebrate strength, heroism, and independence, they have been overshadowed by the chief ideological burden of the poems since the late 1960s: Christianity's guilt for the destruction of the European Jews. In countless poems, buttressed by tough-minded introductory statements to his recent collections, he assumes the stance of prosecutor demanding admission and confession from the Christian world for its culpability in furnishing the theological rationale which, in the course of European history, dehumanized the Jews and ultimately led to the death camps. To his long-standing view of Christianity as perverter of human sexuality and repressive of natural vitality, he now added the direct responsibility for the Holocaust:

> It was Christianity that carefully prepared and seeded the ground on which Europe's gas chambers and crematoria flourished. The beginnings of anti-Semitism are rooted in the mendacious New Testament, where the lie of deicide is forged and foisted on the inhabitants of Judea and succeeding generations of Jews. It was at the Council of Nicea that Jews were officially labelled the murderers of Lord Jesus, and Christians were severely warned against having any commerce with them. It was a pope who invented the Roman ghetto; it was not Hitler but another pope who with Christian charity and tenderness dreamed up the distinguishing yellow Badge of Shame.
>
> The anti-sexuality, anti-life bias at the heart of Christianity contained in its terrible unfolding logic the extermination of

six million human beings. (Foreword, *For My Brother Jesus*, 1976)

Translated to poetry, Layton's accusatory charges are sometimes — as in "For Jesus Christ" — nearly reiterated prose statements:

> One pontiff invented the ghetto;
> more tender and loving, another commanded
> shivering ghosts to wear out its cobblestones
> warmed by the yellow Star of David.

Until the final stanza, where the innocent Jesus is told of the crimes committed in his name in a piercing image which links the related Christian and Nazi symbols, both inescapably implicated as instruments of torture:

> Your stoutest, most selfless partisans in Europe
> laboured nearly two thousand years
> to twist your Cross into the Swastika
> that tore into our flesh like a fish-hook.

In mounting his critique against Christianity, Layton has scrupulously differentiated the historical Jesus from the Church that arose in his name, claiming the former as fellow-Jew and Prophet, while attributing a perverse pathological degeneracy to the latter.

The idea that the teachings of the Jewish Jesus have been misappropriated by the Christians, and that the rightful heirs to his spiritual grace are the Jews, describes Layton's universalistic moralism rather than any consistent religious notions. Certainly, the appropriation of Jesus by the Jews has never been a popular issue amongst Jews, nor has it been espoused in classic or modern Rabbinic literature.

For the poetic act of reclaiming Jesus — among the foremost subjects of his poetry in recent years — does more than merely add one more figure to the pantheon which already includes the writers and thinkers with whom Layton identifies; it also illuminates his conception of Jewish tradition and the true nature of the Jew. Detached from any abiding religious authority, he has assembled a personal tradition, secular in orientation and eclectic in scope. It accommodates the Hebrew prophets and Freud, Spinoza, Heine, and Marx, Jesus and Israeli soldiers, Babel and Mandelstam. From these and other sources he has distilled what he considers their essential Jewish spiritual qualities: unyielding moral purpose, and a heroic assertion of will in the face of human indifference and ignorance. Paradoxically, this synthetic version accords with traditional prophetic narrative which pronounces, time and again, on the fate of the prophet-seers who articulate divine will in order to reform social conduct and spiritual value, and whose exemplary role disturbs the complacency of the majority. But, as Layton sees it, such an account also describes the life of the poet. Being a poet is also to dedicate oneself to a divine calling, to define oneself constantly against the uncomprehending majority, and to contend with the opposition between the poet's visionary insight and the routine reality of the dull-eyed public. In this parallelism between Jewish history and artistic vocation, Layton has found a way of returning to a tradition to which he had been indifferent in his youth. His selective reconstruction of a usable past — judging from the post-1960s poems — has been a potent source of energy from which the inventor of many selves has assumed the guise he had revoked at the beginning of his illustrious career: the self-proclaiming identifiable Jew, eternally troubled and troubling.

Irving and Anna, December 1984.
Photo: David O'Rourke.
Irving Layton Collection, Concordia University.

A SALUTE TO IRVING

Henry Beissel

When I accepted a teaching position in the English Department of Sir George Williams University in 1966, a Toronto friend exclaimed: "That's where Irving Layton teaches, Henry! There isn't room for two explosive people like you in the same department!"

But Irving and I survived — and so did the Department. Now, a quarter of a century later, after who knows how many shared gallons of beer and wine, and the passionate discussions and debates they fuelled, we have developed a friendship that survives even the most serious of spats. Yes, I too have been the recipient of scurrilous postcards; yes, there are sides to Irving's character I could live without — but then could we not all say that of each other? We must accept the world for what it is before we lock horns with it. You cannot have light without shadow, and the brighter the one the darker the other. Besides, the creative process seems to flourish best in a witches' brew of rank muck and turbulent fermentation. And one thing about Irving no one can question is his prodigious, protean creativity.

There are two other qualities that I am sure of and for which I admire him without reservation: his unstinting, generous, bountiful devotion to his students and to any aspiring writer, and his utter, uncompromising, militant commitment to poetry and its central place in any civilization. All of this I know from personal experience, and I can think of no better way to celebrate the man who has written some of the finest poems in this country than by dedicating to him a poem of mine which records a personal experience we both shared, though in very different contexts. "Where Shall the Birds Fly?" records the pain and the shame of one of the most brutal episodes in this brutal century of ours, agonizes over the continuation of our mindless inhumanity, and raises a battle cry on behalf of the world's legions of victims that echoes through all of Irving Layton's poetry. It is only fitting that a poem on which he heaped generous praise should here be offered in praise of him. That the voices of poets shall never fall silent for "In the creative word lies redemption."

HENRY BEISSEL

Where Shall the Birds Fly?

Where can we go on crossing this last border?
Where do birds fly after the final sky?
Where do plants sleep when all the winds have passed?
We write our names in coloured smoke
and we die in this final passage
that olive trees might grow
to mark our place.
— *Mahmoud Darweesh, "Earth Narrows Before Us"*

Who today speaks for that singular remnant
and the desert revelation it gospelled from Moses
to Jesus: love and creativity, freedom from oppression?
I hear only cannons speak, the loudly stuttering Uzzi.
— *Irving Layton, "The Remnant"*

Everywhere the grass is ravishing
the earth, its roots penetrating the dark
to fetch it into the green morning
where a wind warm as blood blows
the light gently into summer's mouth.
Shadows shrink towards the sun
and at its zenith the mind
must measure its own mystery
against the passionate flesh.

    The apple trees are suffering
    their June drop: fruit flawed perhaps
    aborts, the grassgreen matted finish
    beads falling, the rags of wilted
    blossoms still attached to them
    like crippled wings. In the crotch
    of cherry branches tent caterpillars

spin sheets of webbing into layered
transparencies from which they crawl
in languid processions to forage
on young leaves. Silk passage
to the veiled rites of pupation.
Butterflies and moths. A fly catcher
balances on a power line by flip
of tail, surveys the morning's buzz
and hum, then tumbles to a swift dive
to reave bug or beetle from the air.

This is the month Hermes rules,
god of thieves and merchants,
messenger of the gods:
what's the news on high?

The rich are robbing you blind
because there's more money
in bullets than in bread
and they've turned the rains now
into vinegar at the stock market
so they can trade the blue
right out of the sky before you
can paint it the colour of blood.
Tell every broker
the stars are not
for sale. Ask them:

where shall the birds fly
after the final sky?

Arid and breathless, Mercury runs
ellipses round the sun, hugging
its orbit so close that lead melts
at the height of day while its one night
a year is cold enough to liquefy air.
For aeons the heavens cratered
the first planet, each asteroid strike
gouging its face till it was battered

into another lunar wasteland.
But for the relentless wind and the grinding waters,
but for the frost's crowbar and the crunch of continents,
but for the laser sun and the solvents of life,
the metamorphosis of trees and the slow flameless fire
    in the guts of beasts,
    our blue planet too
    would stare at space
    with the empty eyes
    and the savaged face
    of a violent past
    recording a billion-year
    bombardment, the brutal
    expression of a sky
    forever bent on catastrophe.
    The universe conceals
    its chaos from us
    by strategies it programs
    into our retina, turning
    nuclear holocausts
    into ceremonies of gods
    and music, mathematics
    and colour — until once more
    a meteor strikes
    and buries life's
    most daring travellers
    in a millennium of winters.

Summer solstice is close enough
now for a hatching of ant eggs.
Already the devil's paintbrush
is putting orange touches
to the blue air, and black
leaf beetle larvae are gnawing
away the underside of cottonwood
leaves till only the skeletons
of veins are left trembling
on this young season's breath.

And I am condemned to wander
through these woods and fields
backpacking the skeletons
of my childhood. Between
buttercups brimful with golden
light and the plaintive call
of catbirds, over the reed-bending
pond, behind the secretive gestures
of trees, memories hover in search
of a resting-place.

The smell of burning cities, burning flesh
overpowers the pine-scented breeze. I smell fear
and in among aspen leaves I see glittering
stains, always in pairs, small discs shimmering
ovals of light . . . glasses spectacles frames twisted
pince-nez entangled a whole mound of eye-glasses
shattered and askew reflecting a cracked sun eyeless
burning holes in cedar shadows where eyes run over
with pain and terror — whole galaxies of frightened
eyes glow like foxfire in a cankered world.

Behind a Bach concert
in the mind's crimped folds
an evil magic flips
the familiar into a flush
of horror, turning each wood
stand muscular with beeches
into Buchenwald, recalling
the victims in the bluejay's
screeches, and conjuring up
a whole summer full of death
camps for boys and girls.

I hear the howls of men and women
hung from dislocated limbs, swinging
jerking in their sockets I hear shots
bullets thud screaming into flesh
scrupulous not to kill too soon:

Stand to attention,
Schweinhunde!
That's what happens
when you displease
authority power
pride with your con-
duct your convictions
your frailties your genes.
Sing, *Judenlümmel!*
Sing for your life!
All we want is your
watches your gold
teeth your dignity.

Wir werden weiter marschieren . . .
      Is it true is it true
        that we'll march on and on . . .
bis alles in Scherben fällt . . .
      till all the world lies in ruins
. . . *und morgen die ganze Welt*
      till you and I
      are but a charcoal impression
      in a future rock formation?

Where do the twisted trees of hatred grow?
In what polluted soil of the heart?
Is it the acid rain of injustice,
the lethal monoxides of fear
or the pesticides of greed
that nurture them?

   Does someone else's pain
   teach no lessons? What
   about your own?

My memories roar with the fire
storms of Hamburg and Dresden,
linger acrid in the smouldering ruins
of Leningrad and Stalingrad, smell
the macabre sweetness of the smoke

over Birkenau and Belsen —
and now smoke billows over the cities of the Levant:

> O Sidon, jewel of Phoenician cities,
> you traded the treasures of the earth
> and of the sea, your bazaars bargained
> for the envy of kings and queens
> farther back than Babylon. Homer
> sang the praises of your artisans —
> but he knew wealth and beauty
> are the undoing of men and women
> cities and empires: something
> craves to destroy what it cannot
> possess. You were laid to ashes
> by the Philistines and reborn
> from the same stone, turned to ruins
> by Mongols and by Moslems rebuilt
> you were ruled ravaged and restored
> by Assyrians Persians Egyptians
> Romans Arabs Franks and Ottomans
> in the ceaseless tides of history
> till now your ancient walls
> must endure once more
> fire and force of invaders.

Not to dust do we turn
but to ashes. Everything
will burn to ashes.
Everything is born from ashes,
even the inconceivable void
after the final sky.
In another thirty-five sun years
the earth will be a sea
of boiling lava, as our star
burns up its last hydrogen
preparing for the helium flash
that will light the slow fuse
of the final solar pyrotechnics
leaving it a white dwarf
blazing inexorably to cinders.

So the heart is
a fire the sun
ignites in the dark
of carbohydrate tempests
burning us up
in all the colours
the spectrum can mix
between a blinding red
giant and a fugitive
black hole. Solar
flames became flesh
became song in the blood
crucible where life
is freed from slag
and dross to be cast
in the delicate shapes
and patterns of dances,
images, words. Time
in its round-the-clock
laboratory distilled
amino acids into algae,
arthropods, chordates
and worms, each burning
to consume other fires
or be consumed by them
in the advance of flames —
fish, insects, reptiles,
birds and mammals, till
neurons fired in the flesh
its one saving grace: love —
and survival became a ceremony
not a victory:

I love
therefore I am
human.

At summer solstice we used to celebrate
life's pyrotechnics with fireworks of our own:
a giant wheel was rolled flaming into the river

and the night exploded with seedballs of red
shooting-stars and golden rainstorms raging
over song-laden boats and our harmonica
and bonfire hearts dancing garlands of flowers
into a sweeter future. But the cross
that crooked its arms at right angles through
a circle of blood was flexing the muscles
of a reptilian brain crazed and craving
to devour books, cities, innocence and people.
Our summer games turned into gore and thuggery.

> At the edge of the pond
> a nymph is stretched out
> waiting for the sun
> to crack its exoskeleton
> so that from its thorax
> a white-tailed dragonfly
> may emerge. Antlions dig
> circles in fine-grained soil,
> salivate their cocoon snare
> at the bottom of the pit
> and wait with their poison
> to paralyze their prey.
> A solitary bee clambers
> between pistil and stamen
> of a bittersweet, making
> its purpleblue petals tremble
> softly as the thin sibilance
> of mosquitoes drills holes
> into the morning for the past
> to rush in like a horde of harpies.

Where were you
when they smashed babies
against tree trunks?

I was looking for my childhood

when they kicked Jews and Gipsies

I was playing hide-and-seek

trampled Marxists and homosexuals

I was going to be a fireman

till every bone snapped and dreams
ran with blood from mouths noses sex . . .

I was learning history
and sums:
              Multiply the number
              of blind people by
              the number of savages
              and divide by the number
              of innocents: how many
              million corpses do you get?
              The answer is something
              to the power of the power . . .

We were Winnitou and Old Shatterhand
when *SS-Scharführer Sommer*
hung young *Untermenschen*
testicles in boiling water
before tightening the cramp
iron to crack the brain pan.

              O Haupt voll Blut und Wunden . . .

              Suffering has no season
              and bears no fruit.

Where were you?

              I was discovering Bach
              and wet dreams.

Where was I?

I was memorizing verbs dates poems:
amo amas amat amamus . . .
1918 . . . 1933 . . . 1939 . . . *Wer,*
wenn ich schriee, hörte mich denn . . .?

There were no angels winging goodwill
no omniscient gods watching
SS-Oberscharführer Moll line up
women naked by a pit of fire
to target-practice at the bull's eye
the dark triangle of hair:
he had all the angles covered
with blood . . .

    What if
    I had known?
    Would I be here
    to bear witness
    to the pain
    and the shame?

        Lost in the scorched
        and toppled streets
        I was stumbling through
        the ruins of my own
        city not knowing what
        I was looking for what
        I didn't know I was
        looking for
        home.

Home? What home is there
for the eternal wanderer
but a long, dreamless sleep?

        Home is here now
        where memories can get lost
        between summer and northern
        lights, between the shrill

flight of geese and blackfly-
infested   muskegs, between
lashes of snow and the warm
embrace of the Chinook. Here
you can always find a childhood or two by the shore
of a lake or on a prairie
farm a continent and a half
away from the scene
of your nightmares.

Go easy, heart,
on the sleep of prisoners.
The past is a cage
full of pain
and pitfalls.
At different times
different guards
have the same mugs,
the same skulls
in different places
wear the same masks
we call faces.
I recognize them
in the censored newsreels
from Chile and Chicago,
Capetown and Kabul,
Seoul, Moscow and Tel Aviv.
Behind them I see the barbed
wire fences that have become
city limits for refugees,
their faces no-man's land
between exile and existence
in the suburbs of history.

O Tyre, mistress of the Mediterranean,
whose thin-spun silk once limned
the pleasures of Cleopatra — you
withstood Shalmanser and Nebuchadnezzar.

You're at the mercy now of those
who have no mercy: they found the pretext
they were seeking to rape you.

> Gun barrels roar against
> the innocent once more
> to exalt a general's ego,
> once more tanks thunder
> through the cash registers
> of arms manufacturers,
> crushing the hands
> of peasants wresting a home
> from the recalcitrant land,
> and once more planes
> disembowel cities, tearing out
> streets, gutting homes, blast-
> ing whole families to hell
> to swell the bosoms of god's
> chosen, the Swiss accounts
> of wheelers and dealers
> relaxing before breakfast
> in a warm bloodbath:

Tyre, Sidon, Damur, Beirut —
the peace of Galilee
is a web of lies. Black
smoke sears and surges
as once above Warsaw
and Cologne — a warning signal
to the heavens that on this planet
we burn all that is human
in the crematoriums
of our messianic fantasies.
Ashes, ashes everywhere.

> Does it matter
> when everything
> is burning
> to ashes, when
> even matter itself is mortal?

Each proton decays
into an anti-electron
seeking to encounter
an electron jointly
to vanish without
a trace in a burst
of gamma rays.

What place the heart
where you and I add up
to zero? What of the mind
when all the possible worlds
have run round two or three
dozen zeros till there is
nothing left but nothing?

Lend me your ears, fearful
captive reader, I can smell you
as far back as the primal soup,
even under the rain of ashes
drifting through this maple
and spruce forest. I want you
to listen to the sunlight
stalking shadows on moccasined feet
and to the grass converting dung
into blossoms. Watch the bright
pink pouches of the lady's slipper
rise from acid bogs to lure the bumblebee
to push apart the veined lips and enter into
the ancient trade of nectar for pollen.
Insects make the world burst into flower:
the whole spectacle of colours
and the raptures of scent are but to entice
and seduce them — an arabesque of the senses
to embellish survival strategies,
a Bach fugue chasing its own flight
in the cave dwellings of the heart.

This is the month Franklin
perished in the ice
on his passage northwest
where even the wind came
black and ravenous
to the frozen camp
to lick their bones clean.
It is the month Kafka
died, begging his friend
to burn the record
of his nightmare journeys.
They braved the void
and found an end
in their travels.

Energy creates worlds from nothing
in the emptiness which makes movement
possible: space is an invitation to move
to keep a rendezvous with time.
Electrons flashing erratically
at 600 m.p.s. about their core
make stone endure and timber hold,
unleash the wind against mountains
and cast whole continents into the sea,
temper the stars into distances
and enforce a cold and eerie silence
upon a lunar night. They excite
the cell to divide symmetrically,
wrap the velvet flesh around their own
contrivances of blood and bone,
and stir the mind to music and murder.

In the molecular dance of the universe
the hall too dances and the floor spins,
yet we are the dancing-masters
of our destiny.

We are
what we do
with what we are.

Put your ear to the ground
and check your pulse against
the earth's dark heart. Summer
is an invitation to lie naked
in the grass and let the green
fingers of the sun brush all
sorrow from your flesh. The wild
irises unfurl their blue
flags and ants climb through
hedge bindweed into the morning
glories trumpeting the golden
silence of approaching noon into thickets
where deep in the weeds a song
sparrow broods speckled eggs
on a moss-lined nest while its mate
chirps and trills as sprightly
as the light is long.

A flute, a badinerie,
a Bach suite — moment
of sheer joy dancing
through the open window
of an improbable
world where at any time
jet fighter planes thousands
of miles away can scream
into your eyes and scare up
memories thousands of years
back in your own childhood:

Searchlights — bony fingers
combing the night sky,
skeletal hands plucking enemy
planes from a black drone,
basements sandbagged, stifling

with the smell of urine and fear,
air raid shelters, astringent
taste of damp grit, the short bark
of anti-aircraft guns, the swift
downscale glissando of the bomb
that missed you, and after a heart-
stopping hesitation the fortissimo
reaffirmation of your existence
breaking every window cracking
every wall for blocks, detonations
with enough decibels to rupture
your eardrums and decades later
still devastate your cochlea.
The awesome silence that follows
is ashen, whimpering and sobbing
with plaster in their hair
mothers age in seconds, their
children big-eyed, torn between
terror and adventure, choking
on cement dust and
the incomprehensible
madness of this man-
made apocalypse.

I have been there
and come back.
I have seen
the children
the bombs
didn't miss:

  a bundle of bandages wound
  immaculately like a fresh mummy
  with a single slot for the mouth
  where the nurse slips in
  the bottle to feed
  the napalm-fried infant.

Or the nine-year-old, shredded
by a cluster bomb, both legs
and testicles blown off, looking
at night for his itching feet.

Atura hal junna hissi?
Are my senses mad?

> The harpsichord is lost now
> in the woodlands of Glengarry
> the last chord skimming silver-footed
> across a stagnant pond. A flicker
> chiselling rapid-fire a dead elm
> is gentler than the images
> drilling into my heart's core.

A twelve-year-old, skull
and spine broken under the rubble
of her home, her left ear black
and silent, her left eye blind
with blood, her damaged brain dreaming
of life as a ballerina.

> Huda, Ahmad, Wafa —
> why is it my childhood
> memories have Arab names?

Sometimes there are pictures
from Lebanon that bear
names from my childhood:
Klaus, Inge, Lech, Kasis, Mordecai —
  You cannot hear me
  though I testify
  on your behalf.

I heard the general declare: "Why should we
distinguish between civilians
and soldiers? No one can teach us
to be human." — Who said that?

Heinrich, Jarek, Menachem?
How to distinguish
yesterday from today
when no lessons are learnt?

Suffering is not a function
of numbers, but of pain.

Is this defenseless city
Warsaw or Beirut?
Bombed and shelled
into a lunar wasteland,
climax to a *Blitzkrieg*
against the unarmed,
last act of the *Götterdämmerung*
of some deluded *Herrenvolk*.

Joshua fought the battle of Jericho
and the walls came tumbling down.

Carthago delenda est.

Wir werden ihre Städte ausradieren!

Is this a true audit
of history, certified
by the chartered accountants
of our aspirations? I know
the generals ordering food
and water supplies cut off
are the same who own shares
in arms and munitions, but
are the soldiers the patients
in the hospitals they shell,
the teachers in the schools
they burn? The same puppets
pulled by the same strings
of money, slogans and pride
in this global village theatre
of profit and loss? Listen:

Of the cities of these people
thou shalt save alive nothing
that breathes: thou shalt
utterly destroy them!

Thus spake Yahweh
in a testament that is holy
only to a species surrendering
any claim to the future.

The cockroach can survive
without mythologies
levels of radiation
that will exterminate us.

Are we to be
executioners
merely
of arithmetic
sentences
the cosmos passes
on all and sundry
predictably
at random?
Marionettes,
you and I,
in a nuclear theatre,
blocked by forces
weak and strong,
gravity and
electromagnetic waves,
destined for the scrapheap
of a preposterous history?
All of us victims
of our own mythologies?

Every child is a future
where a man or a woman
can be free and equal.

Chosen people make terror
reasonable and love
impossible.

> Confined to chance
> orbits halfway
> to the stars
> you and I are charged
> with self-perpetuating,
> like electrons circling
> hectically the dead
> centre of life, moving
> in the emptiness only
> an embrace can endure.

In the mountains of the Lebanon
where rivers once fierce have cut
deep valleys tortured to the sea
I hear six-year old Bandali sing:

> Give me back my laughter
> give me back my doll
> give me back my childhood
> give me back my home.

Her childish voice echoes inside me
louder than the banging and bellowing of war.
It carries the burden of its elegy on the back
of pastured slopes, drifts down meandering
streams, lingers in olive orchards or over
the aromatic elegance of cypress trees,
a song looking for deliverance in sacred
groves where a gentler god once raised cedars
majestic from the ground to stand arms outstretched to bless the beauty of this land.

> Can a jet-fighter pilot
> on a supersonic reconnaissance
> mission hear the song or

identify the cedars,
smell the eucalyptus?

Our humanity is
an inverse function
of the speed
at which we pass
each other.

The train's whistle sounds wild
and doleful across the apple trees,
like the howl of a wolf desperate
to be heard in another dimension.
It hurtles towards noon oblivious
of the colonies of wild blue phlox
bending to the pressure wave,
of the squirrels mating in the pine
and the tachinid fly that oviposits
behind the head of a caterpillar,
its larvae parasites destined to devour
their host. Again and again the train
howls shuttling drowsy travellers
between a handful of cities spared
the sound of bombs except in the sleep
of those who cannot forget or forgive —

while across an ocean and a half the Hasbani
still carries the last stars downstream,
and grey-haired Mt. Hermon, *Jabal al-shaykh*,
looks eastward waiting for Castor and Pollux
to fetch dawn shivering from faraway deserts.
Westward in the direction of the sea
the night is bleeding into dark
valleys beneath a horizon on fire.

How can you tell
one burning image
from another through
the prism of your tears?

The Warsaw ghetto or
a Palestinian refugee camp?
Photos from a doomsday book:

/ *a group of women, an old man,*
children, their arms raised
in surrender to the uniforms of
gun-toting terror, in their midst
a small girl stunned in her mother's
skirt, a muskrat paralyzed with fear
in a steel trap /

    / *teachers, scientists, artists*
    blindfolded, roped together like
    camels, stumbling through ruins:
    "all of a sudden they are
    a bunch of nothings"
    the victors' caption reads /

        / a mother lifts
        her dead child
        bloodspattered
        to high heaven
        with a piercing
        wail that should
        move the stars /

Is this the way the world ends
— in Warsaw and Treblinka
in a blaze of firestorms and furnaces
incinerating all that is gentle and good
— in Sabra and Shatila
in the glare of magnesium flares
lighting up the night officially
for a massacre of innocents?

        Atura hal junna hissi?
        I hear the poet sing
        Khalil's pain I hear

the shot ring out the shame
Khalil's pride I hear
the bullet sever the song
from the blood of Khalil
who would not sing
after the fall of the city
had driven his senses mad.

Where shall the birds fly
after the final sky?

Onehundredandsixtythreethousand
light years ago in the Large
Magellanic Cloud a giant star
collapsed under its own gravity
until its iron core caught
fire and blew apart, ejecting
its elements into space
with enough energy to incinerate
any nearby solar system
and seed new ones farther away.
Among stars birth is
like death a cataclysm
without survivors. Only
onehundredandsixtythreethousand
light years away is a supernova
a spectacle to delight the awed
mind on the threshold of madness.

I lie in the moist grass trying
to banish the ghosts of yesteryear
from the dishevelled circle of clouds
where even a friendly face drifts
too lightly into a grimace. Down
here the grotesque air is green
and the earth's dampness cools
the troubled shades. A spittlebug nymph
is drinking alfalfa upside down
from a plant stalk, converting sap

into a froth cocoon. It has no receptors
for the rush of music skipping
with measured step between blades of grass
and round wildflower stems, impetuous
as some long-repressed need for joy
and affirmation, bursts of strings and brass
chasing each other through baroque tangles
of underbrush till they drop out of hearing
in the somber corridors of the bush.
Are the bees dancing to Bach
among the clover — or is it only
my thoughts, my fancy, this summer
saraband in an alien land?

    A swarm of redpolls puts some colour
    in the hemlock tree. I hoist myself
    into the tall day, leaning on their chatter,
    and scare up a groundhog. Stretched high
    on its hindlegs, it eyes me, rigid
    as a taxidermist's pose, except it cannot
    stop munching. Fat and devious
    it devours the sprouts of peas,
    beans, spinach, the whole gourd family
    buds . . . — Rage explodes in the dark
    and convoluted spaces of my skull
    and hurls murder into my eyes . . .
    I take aim, my index finger crooks
    for a trigger —

Is this the passion
that turns Ariel
into a butcher
and makes a mockery
of every Bach chorale?
The alien intruder
threatening our dreams?

        In days of fear gods bless night
        and bombs. In the territories

of fear an eye calls
for an eye and the clenched fist
promises peace and money
is the measure of our love.

But you cannot buy the stars
and if you sell a brother or sister
you have invested in a holocaust.
The world's battlefields are quagmires
of blood and guts that have sucked
heroes and cowards alike to their foul
deaths, the naïve and the fanatic
perishing with their pain in the torture
chambers of history as nations, races
and religions take turns at being victims
and victimizers in orgies of slaughter
and sacrifice madmen organize
to maintain the privileges
of those who have not
earned them.

Russians Germans Arabs
and Jews, Christians
Muslims Fascists —
all labels tell you
is the disease:
        xenophobic epilepsy
        ideological elephantiasis
        messianic carcinoma
        the master-race syndrome . . .

Can the sun
can anything
save us
cure us
from ourselves?

June is the month that lights up
the north from horizon to horizon

stretching the days more than halfway
around the globe, growing galaxies
in the leaves of every tree, hatching
schools of sun in every ocean breaker,
placing a sun on the wing of every bird
and insect, the tip of every reed
and grass, in the belly of every drop
of rain and in the hearts of all
who flounder between fear and fulfillment.

    Skeletons under the skull
    dance in darkness and reach
    for light in the retina.
    I come away with
    only an eye full
    of images:

                the three-year-old
                with her throat cut,
                the castrated boy,
                women raped, piles
                of mutilated bodies,
                a bulldozer manoeuvering
                with shovel full of corpses
                starved till the parched skin
                could barely hold the knobbed
                bones, harrowed till the mind
                could no longer endure living
                the pain the living pain of
                dying the pain the stars
                cannot know the pain . . .

This pain too, like all we know,
joins the procession of memories
that move peristaltically
in the pilgrimage of San Isidro
Goya painted in the Quinta del Sordo
across the scorched landscape of this age.
Enterrar y callar. I cannot

bury them and be silent. I hear
the voices, the endless march
of prisoners and victims —
victims of war, prisoners of lies,
victims of conscience, prisoners
of fear: they drag the chains
of grief and guilt down the blood
tracks across the sands of this century.

> *No business like shoah business.*
> *Shoah business is no business.*

A carnival parade led by the king of fools
surrounded by blind musicians and pious
time servers: they award the peace prize
to a terrorist on a float of booby-traps.
The banner reads: ONLY VIOLENCE CAN PUT AN END
TO VIOLENCE. Black uniforms goose-step faceless
behind a blond doll carrying a pirate's flag and
repeating in a shrill, mechanical voice:

> black is white
> might is right —
> pick your enemy and fight!
> Have your fill
> make your kill —
> war is money in the till!
> Better dead
> than pink or red —
> there's no more to be said!

Para eso habéis nacido.
Is that what we were born for?
A cradle made from barbed wire
and in it the torso of a girl
     singing:

> *give me back my laughter*
> give me back my doll

give me back my childhood
give me back my home.

Tears wash the eyes
but they blur the vision.
They make old wounds
burn without washing
the past off your hands.
You can build a house
on the ruins of someone else's,
but you can find no home there.

Yesterday's Jew is
today's Palestinian.

Every refugee camp
cries out bears witness
against us — in Pakistan,
Sri Lanka, Vietnam, Chile
and Honduras, in Mozambique,
Namibia and the Sudan,
in Jordan and Lebanon —
we've driven millions
from their homes into
a world of camps where
children die of diarrhea
and the destitute receive
their dignity as handouts
in shantytowns. The dream
of universal brotherhood
lies shattered in tin can
shacks and cardboard tents.
History is wasted
on a people who survive
only to inflict their own
persecutions on others
in a single generation.

Not that you fiddle your suffering
from every rooftop makes you human
but that you bury vengeance
in the barbaric caves of your heart.

    Beirut is burning.
    Palestine's people
    are on the move again
    looking for home.
    Where shall the birds fly
    after the final sky?

A dream is burning to the ground
and from the ashes rises the raven
of separation to pitch its caws
across the river where Tammuz' blood
flows still through the valleys of Hasbaya.
The raven flies black and shrill
through fig orchards and pomegranate groves,
its shrieks sharp knives to stab the hearts
of mourners weeping and wailing in red-
roofed villages for the dead who wanted
nothing but a home. Jerusalem, cradle

  of three faiths,
  and not one gesture
  of grace to trade
  in Beirut's kidnapping
  bazaars against
  an innocent victim
  or cut the barbed
  wire between the two
  cities where it's easier
  for mountains to meet
  than for an eye
  to encounter an eye
  without shame.

    Your shame is my shame
    and my shame is your shame.

Reflected ghostly in the window
my eyes stare me in the face,
burning with the shame of being
human. A feisty crow freefalls
from the top of the spruce tree,
a bold black slash across my mouth.
It banks against the cedar-shingled
roof with a scream alarming enough
to scare away the plaintiffs from
my childhood, and plunges headlong
into the bush vanishing between
wildly staggered soft-edged planes
of green and grey on wings wafting
calmly like large pine branches
awash with shade and silence.

      And suddenly the light is
      as golden as the many yellows
      into which van Gogh painted
      his sitters, his flowers,
      his fields. A flock of evening
      grosbeaks flutters into maple trees,
      their white tertiaries flashing
      as they dance from branch to branch
      agitated by a music I cannot hear.
      Perhaps the spheres sing for them
      to make a midsummernight's dream
      come true. A rabbit sits erect
      and scoops up a tall earful
      of this hour's hums and whirs
      whispers rustles and cracks
      trills plashes sighs clicks
      guggles smacks purls and swishes —

Who could've dreamt the bang
that rent a vacuum and smashed
eternal darkness into spacetime
would ever cool down to the temper
of so faint and fragile a music

as orchestrates the balletomania of life.
Who could've dreamt the many worlds
compressed into a sphere of quarks
less than a billionth of an attosecond
old and no bigger than a Mackintosh apple,
a mere bite from which would've contained
all the galaxies and stars, all the nebulae,
gases, quasars and black holes, travelling
time immemorial at the speed of an explosion
away from a centre so small it would've fitted
in the palm of your hand. Who could've dreamt
the sun, the moon and our bluegreen planet
in that dense bubble of catastrophic patterns
of energy — the potential for every possible
reality, including you and me, our struggles,
whether won, lost or ever engaged in, all that
we might have been and will never be, all
the journeys we might have taken plus the one
we do complete, all that packed into one
Hot Big Bang the size of a baseball
that threw billions of universes curved
across billions of light years of space.

    Farewell, unquiet memories,
    the shadows are too slim now
    to sustain you. The sun
    in its zenith lights up
    an inner eye. June is
    the month John Cabot first
    caught sight of this old
    continent, dreaming of jewels,
    spices and gold, aboard a ship
    no larger than a human heart
    and crammed full of worlds
    and dreams wanting to explode
    and hurl galaxies of joy
    into the dark and brutal spaces
    between persecution and war,
    new worlds not waiting for

discoverers but for creators
inspired by the possibilities
of light. Only gods
can afford to make
an ass of love.

I emerge from the chrysalis of memory
to reach out across half a century
to touch you, my unknown friend,
and your pain in the camps of death.
And I stretch my hands to reach across
an ocean and a sea to beat the durbakki
drums alongside a young man in a refugee camp
in the mountains of the Levant. Together
we strike up the dabka dance, ancient circle
of lives more enduring than the walls
of cities or the cruel arts of invaders.

Goldfinches flit through thorn bushes.
Deep in the forest calypso orchids
bloom magenta, their clusters of stamen
tiny bursts of sunlight in the cool shade.
A pair of sulphur butterflies spiral up
and down about each other, rising higher
and higher till they're dancing on tree tops
and the male abruptly plumps down swift
and bright as a meteor, followed by
the fluttering caprice of the female,
a lotus blossom floating down to her
palpitating mate in the low creeping
grass where a killdeer drags its unbroken
wing with cries of alarm theatrically
away from its nest from its young from
its dupe till it is safe to break free.

Up north in the Truelove Lowlands
on Devon Island musk oxen shed their underfur
among the emerging bluegrass, foxtail and willow
herbs; they stand their desolate frozen ground

against men and wolves shoulder to shoulder
in a dark rosette — a primordial circle
that has kept ice ages and predators at bay.

IRVING LAYTON AND MARXISM: AN INTERVIEW

Ekbert Faas with Maria Trombacco

The following questions take into account whatever has been written about Irving Layton's political life and ideas by himself and by others; and although the interview does not take such knowledge for granted, it tries to fill in the gaps and touch on controversial issues rather than retrace what is known already.

LAYTON

Let me read "Sunflowers," my tribute to Herr Marx. It will establish the mood for our talk.

How majestic they were
a brief month ago, tall-erect;
now bare but for petals
that reach out like begging hands.

Blind Oedipus and his companion,
they lean against the air
and mock the betraying sun.

The morning glory's faded beauty
is no comfort, nor the white ash of my cigar.
I know what I know. Everything flows;
living, dies: the intruding dog in my garden,
the butterflies cavorting
over the plundered mounds. The white disaster
is on the way
and will not be stopped.

I think of the young Marx,
heaven-storming Promethean, making
kings and capitalists quake
with his *Grundrisse*, his black smouldering eyes
— praising unalienated man, Superman!

"I sowed dragons' teeth and reaped pygmies."

No, my red Messiah, tempestuous Jew.
Your sunflower beauty still flourishes,
astonishes; still rouses man-enslaved man,
poet and mad philosopher
at noonday and in the stillest hour of the night.

QUESTION

In *Waiting for the Messiah* you have described the evolution of your political ideas until about 1945. What has happened since then?

LAYTON

I would say that I am more thoroughly Marxist now than I've ever been. I am quite convinced that capitalism is a sick system. It's dying on its legs. It's a corpse, and it's becoming a stinking corpse. And it has to be destroyed, it has to be gotten rid of. There's a "bourgeois decadence" now, just as there used to be an aristocratic, feudal decadence. There's evidence of it everywhere. All you have to do is breathe in deeply and get the smell of it.

QUESTION

Even in the affluent countries?

LAYTON

Especially in the affluent countries. Because that's their only ideology. Their only ideology is to make money and to get ahead and so on and so forth.

QUESTION

Meanwhile, you have criticized notions like the 'dictatorship of the proletariat' as wrong-headed and obsolete.

LAYTON

I don't think that Marx himself was interested in that except as a temporary sort of thing.

QUESTION

So what would you retain as the essence of Marxism?

LAYTON

The criticism of the capitalist system. And the organization of a party dedicated to change, and to eliminating the capitalist system. First of all through education, then through the newspapers, the writers, the universities and colleges. They all have to inculcate the idea that capitalism is a foul system, whose time to go has now arrived. And the longer we delay that the worse it will be for mankind.

QUESTION
When I recently visited Manaus in Brazil and took a bus trip just outside town, I was struck to see all the big corporations from Japan, Europe, the United States, and next to them, the garrisons with the Brazilian military there to protect the corporate interests against the Brazilian people. There's sufficient evidence from recent history that that's how it works. It's like an ultimate anonymity of evil. And yet you have argued that the international corporations are functioning as peace makers.[1]

LAYTON
I'm not denying what you say. I'm no lover of the international corporations at all. But look what's happened to the world. They've gotten rid of the nuclear menace. And why is that? Precisely because Japanese, American, and European capitalists now are more concerned with trade than they are with making war.

QUESTION
In 1967 you wrote: "we have discovered we have a better system [than the communists]: the price system . . . that permits us . . . a great amount of liberty . . ."[2]

LAYTON
I think the failure of the Soviet Union happened because they had no price system at all. What they had instead was a command system which fosters bribery, corruption, and inefficiency. But there's no reason why a socialist society couldn't be run on a price system. As long as it's properly operated.

QUESTION
So that's why state socialism has failed around the world?

LAYTON
It failed for two reasons. It failed first of all because it didn't have a price system. And secondly because the socialists, and that includes Marx, didn't have a very deep understanding of human nature.

QUESTION
How is that?

LAYTON
They failed to understand that there is a desire for power. And that there's greed. The desire for power and greed are two powerful human motivations. They overlooked that. And the experience with Stalin and Stalinism shows precisely how corrupt human nature can be, especially when it has the disguise of idealism — in the same way in which Christianity used to mask the basest motivations. This is very natural. But we now know a little more about human nature because of Nietzsche, Freud, and psychoanalysis. We know a lot more than Marx knew. After all Marx lived before Freudianism and psychoanalysis.

QUESTION
And yet Marx wasn't exactly what you'd call an optimist with regard to human nature. There's an almost Schopenhaurian streak in him. I guess he just never thought it through.

LAYTON
I couldn't agree with you more.

QUESTION
I'd like to retrace your origins and general development as a Marxist. It's been suggested that an early influence here came from your brother Abraham's reading the Montreal Yiddish papers disseminating communist ideals.[3]

LAYTON
Abraham had no importance at all because my brother could read Yiddish and I couldn't. So I didn't read the newspapers he read. I never heard Abraham talk about socialism or Marx. I would very much doubt that he was interested in either.

QUESTION
How about your brother-in-law Benny Cohen who, when you were a kid, threw around names like Marx, Kropotkin, and Lassalle.

LAYTON
Benny Cohen was just a loudmouth who liked to show off. Proudhon, that was another one. He would throw around names rather

than ideas. I don't remember his ever having talked about ideas.

QUESTION
So again, there was no influence on you?

LAYTON
Not the slightest.

QUESTION
So the first to really introduce you to Marx were Suzanne Rosenberg and her mother.

LAYTON
Both Suzanne and her mother were communists. Suzanne was a YCLer [member of the Young Communist League] and her mother was a member of the Communist Party. Since I wooed them and liked them and saw them quite frequently, I would hear words like 'historical and dialectical materialism,' 'profit,' 'the price system,' or even 'capitalism.' It's with them that I first heard 'capitalism' used as a term of abuse and invective. So they gave me the emotional idea of what communism was all about. But I might add that it was at David Lewis' Young People's Socialist League that I may have picked up a lot of other concepts such as 'surplus value,' 'exploitation,' and perhaps even the 'class struggle.'

QUESTION
You have said that David Lewis succeeded where the Rosenbergs had failed in trying to turn you into a communist, and that socialism as a result began to replace the faith of your forefathers.[4]

LAYTON
David Lewis was several years older than I and knew a great deal about socialism, so I admired him. He was a very persuasive speaker. But the statement you quote carries an unavoidable ambiguity that needs clearing up. There is a difference between socialists and communists. Both have as their goal the establishment of a socialist system, but they differ in their strategies. The communists lost me when they proposed to reach the goal of socialism through violence, while David Lewis suggested that we could attain it democratically. So it was he who won me over to that broader socialist ideal to be achieved by peaceful means.

QUESTION

From early on you'd quarrelled with the kind of communism the Rosenbergs stood for. At some point in talking to Suzanne you called Lenin "a murderous Tartar."[5]

LAYTON

That was my first real argument, I won't say quarrel, with Suzanne. She started to sob and I tried to console her. I took her into my arms and apologized profusely for calling her idol a murderer. There was a picture of Lenin in their house.

QUESTION

What texts of Marx and Engels did the Rosenbergs make you read?

LAYTON

The Communist Manifesto, of course; then the book on Feuerbach which was the first to throw light for me on what 'Capitalism' was all about; also Marx's *The Class Struggles in France*, a very important and seminal book, which introduced me to Marx's theories about 'historical materialism.' From these I went on to Lenin's *Imperialism*.[6]

QUESTION

At that point?

LAYTON

Oh yes.

QUESTION

What else by Lenin?

LAYTON

I also looked at his *Empirio-criticism*[7], but that was beyond me at the time. My philosophical background wasn't deep enough to appreciate what Lenin was getting at. But I certainly read his *Imperialism* as well as many of his manifestoes, also the book on *Left-Wing Communism*.[8] It's Lenin's persistent criticism of social democracy that helped to wean me from reformist socialism. I also read Trotsky.

QUESTION

His *History of the Russian Revolution*?

LAYTON

I read that. But above all I was interested in his literary criticism, his ideas about a revolutionary literature.[9] I found that very stimulating.

QUESTION

At the same time, you started to read a lot of twentieth-century Marxist or socialist writers.

LAYTON

Yes, those first two years or so were very formative years — the ideas gripped me very passionately.

QUESTION

You've listed some of the authors you then read, such as V.F. Calverton, Granville Hicks, Grace Lumpkin, Michael Gold, or Howard Fast, now mostly forgotten. Are there any texts among these you'd ever return to?

LAYTON

No. None.

QUESTION

How about Marx himself?

LAYTON

That's different. Marx I've read all my life and I still do. I come back to him again and again, always with deeper understanding.

QUESTION

Which texts of his do you prefer?

LAYTON

I like his pamphlets and I particularly admire his historical books, like *The Eighteenth Brumaire of Louis Napoleon* and *The Class Struggles in France*.

QUESTION

How about *The Holy Family*?

LAYTON

I've read that more recently.

QUESTION

Or *The German Ideology*?

LAYTON

Yes, I even read *The German Ideology*. But that was later, when I got interested in philosophy and Marxism concurrently.

QUESTION

How about Lenin? Would you still go back to reading him like Marx?

LAYTON

Oh definitely. Books like his *Left Wing Communism* or his *One Step Forward, Two Steps Back* are cardinal works.

QUESTION

How about Laski?

LAYTON

No, I wouldn't look at Laski now because he was not a profound thinker. He was more of a stylist than a thinker.

QUESTION

Or Robert Owen's *New View of Society*?

LAYTON

Once again, Owen was not an original thinker like Marx was; he's not in that class at all. He'd be *passé* for me now.

QUESTION

You remember how Suzanne attacked you for being a "renegade socialist" and "cowardly revisionist."[10] That would have been in the late twenties. Now at a later point, around 1946, that's precisely the kind of terminology you will use to criticize Laski in your M.A. thesis. And Lenin, whom you earlier called a "murderous Tartar," now becomes one of your mentors. In fact, it's Lenin's attack on the German socialist Kautsky which you now use to criticize Laski.

LAYTON

Precisely.

QUESTION

So there's a major change in outlook.

LAYTON

That's because I began to see the weaknesses in social democracy. I felt that the communists' critique of the capitalist and imperialist systems and their understanding of the nature of the class struggle was much deeper, more pertinent, and sharper than that of the social democrats. For that reason I turned away from McDonaldism and social democracy and a belief in the Labour Party, or later the NDP, as a means for the transformation of society.

QUESTION
And you did so in spite of the fact that you knew about the Stalinist purges.

LAYTON
Yes, later I began to see the weaknesses and atrocities of that system. But at that time I wasn't thinking too deeply about Stalin or Stalinism. So, instead, I began to disagree with social democracy because I realized that it did not aim at a complete up and down reconstruction of society which is what Marx wanted. Not just a tinkering around with it.

QUESTION
The old quarrel between Marx and Lassalle.

LAYTON
Exactly. And I stuck with Marx. For me it was merely a matter of finding the right interpreter for Marx. Well, the communists came along and put forth Lenin as that, and for a while I accepted him. But later on I realized that Lenin had degraded Marx, just as Stalin had degraded Lenin.

QUESTION
In which sense?

LAYTON
In the sense of giving Marxism a totalitarian colour.

QUESTION
That's Rosa Luxemburg's critique of Lenin.

LAYTON
You see, Lenin was a Russian, was a Byzantine with his idea of a welding of the church and state, or of the Communist Party and society.

QUESTION
So your criticism of Laski whom you'd praised so highly earlier had

nothing to do with your trying to please your thesis supervisors?

LAYTON
I never tried to please anybody.

QUESTION
Were you influenced by your supervisors? I'm thinking of Raphael Tuck, Frank Scott, or Eugene Forsey?

LAYTON
Not at all. It's all part of *my* thinking.

QUESTION
How did they like the thesis?

LAYTON
Tuck, my actual supervisor, wanted to get me an 'A.' He definitely thought it was first rate work. But Scott would only give me a pass, so that's what I got. I suspect that's because Scott was definitely CCF [Co-operative Commonwealth Federation], while my own attitude had become more Leninist in its critique of the social democracy which he stood for.

QUESTION
Did you ever join the Communist Party?

LAYTON
I was never a member of the Communist Party. I was never even a member of the YCL [Young Communist League].

QUESTION
Were you ever drawn to a Bakunin-Nechaev type anarchism?

LAYTON
No, never.

QUESTION
Yet while you lived in Halifax you seem to have been associated with a communist 'cell.'

LAYTON
They wanted me to join them but I didn't. We took these long walks on the waterfront because we didn't want the RCMP or anyone else to overhear us. And I told them definitely that I wouldn't become a member of the party because I did not agree with their conspiratorial

tactics. I also disagreed with their saying that the Second World War and Canada's role in it were essentially imperialist like the First. My response to that was that the Second World War was a necessary and legitimate war against Germany and its fascism. In fact, I myself enlisted in it and was commissioned as an officer.

QUESTION

I'd like to briefly come back to your involvement with the CCF and David Lewis. From being a mentor and friend, who at one point gave you ten dollars so you could write your junior matrics at McGill, David Lewis later turned into a person blocking your getting a job with the CCF, suggesting that you were a kind of communist in disguise trying to infiltrate that federation.[11]

LAYTON

David Lewis was a good socialist and he believed in evolution, reform, and parliamentary democracy. I agreed with him that we want ballots rather than bullets. But I also wanted to see a complete change in social, economic and political relationships. I accepted Marx's main idea of the emancipation of the working class. That idea appealed to me thoroughly. And behind that the Marxist notion of a complete change in the social system. So I was never more than a fellow traveller of David Lewis' type of socialism. Eventually my criticism of socialism and social democracy reached the ears of the CCF and the Young Peoples' Socialist League. So I became suspect to them. They were also suspicious of my pro-Soviet stance; for instance, there'd be an open public meeting to protest some police brutality in Montreal and I'd be one of the speakers. And in my speech, I'd wander off a bit from the speech I'd prepared to say some complimentary things about the Soviet Union. At that time I accepted the thesis that the capitalist states would like to destroy the Soviet Union. And as a believer in Marxism, I thought that it was the duty of all radicals of whatever political persuasion to defend the Soviet Union. And I said so. That didn't go down very well with the socialists, didn't go down very well with the CCF. And from that point on they ostracized me because they thought I was an enemy of theirs and even some kind of agent of the Communist Party.

QUESTION

Did you ever actually try to infiltrate the CCF?

LAYTON

No, not at all. I never even tried to join the CCF. Why would I have wanted to? Because I repudiated that whole ideology. Also, I wouldn't join any organization for a dishonest, hypocritical purpose. If I wanted to destroy somebody or something, I would do it openly. That's my *métier*. I don't hide behind anything. What I applied for at the time, when David Lewis wrote that letter about me, was an educational job which had some kind of connection with the socialist movement. In other words, I was very interested in spreading socialist ideas in general (i.e., sociology, economics and historical thought), but never in joining the CCF.

QUESTION

So what political groups did you actually belong to?

LAYTON

I was a member of the Young Peoples' Socialist League — we called them Yippsels. In fact, I was one of their co-founders. Then I was a member of the Youth Defenders which was a fake organization, a mere front for the Communist Party, which I didn't know then. I was never a member of the Young Communist League. But I'd meet them at Murray's and other restaurants on Main Street in Montreal. I found them quite unsympathetic temperamentally in their dogmatism even then. I also met with the Trotskyites. I just loved debate and argument. Most of these groups had their meeting places on Main Street, between Pine and Mount Royal. Or at Horn's. If you walked in there and had the price for a cup of coffee, which was a nickel, you could have the most wonderful discussions with an assortment of radicals. That in effect was my university. That's where I got my training.

QUESTION

What is your view of present-day NDP policies?

LAYTON

Well, of the political parties in Canada, you might say that the NDP should be favoured. But the NDP is so ineffectual. If I'm going to support a political party, I'd like to know that I can get something out of it, from it, and through it. And I don't think I can get anything from the NDP. On the other hand, I believe that I can get something out of the Liberal Party. So at the present juncture in history, I would support the Liberal Party.

QUESTION

The NDP seems to be creating a welfare state which will help ruin the country financially.

LAYTON

Well I'm not interested in welfarism. I'm interested in socialism.

QUESTION

A socialism in which everybody is active instead of being encouraged to live off welfare.

LAYTON

Right. There's been a degradation of real socialism into welfarism. And I'm opposed to that.

QUESTION

Rereading your various essays, we found that the Cuban Missile Crisis marks a decided change in your attitude to the U.S.S.R. Even during the previous spy plane incident of 1960 your sympathies were with "the Russian people in this new hour of trial and anxiety, so callously provoked by the U.S." But then in 1962, when you send a letter to President Kennedy, you suddenly come out strongly in support of the United States.[12] And from then on you hail the U.S. as the main opponent . . .

LAYTON

. . . of Soviet communism, which I came to regard as the main threat to mankind.

QUESTION

So there was a radical change at this point?

LAYTON

Definitely. And I speak openly about that in various essays and articles. It's when I saw the fight looming up between the U.S.A. and the U.S.S.R., that I took my stand unequivocally on the side of America. It seemed to me that only America, and I said so, could halt the triumphant march of Soviet-style communism. And therefore I went all out for Kennedy, Johnson, and so forth. Because for me the most important issue was the defeat of the Soviet Union, the defeat of Soviet communism. And I don't regret that one single bit.

QUESTION

In 1963, upon the publication of your *Balls for a One-Armed Juggler*, your old friend Desmond Pacey accused you of having lost your Marxism. To which you replied that you were as Marxist as ever.[13] So you seem to distinguish between the state socialism of the East Bloc countries and Marxism as an ideology at that point.

LAYTON

That's right. But it took me a little while before I understood the essence of Marxism. And that I've remained faithful to right up until now. It's the most radical criticism of society and civilization ever put forward by the mind of man. And it aims at the emancipation of mankind. It makes man the hope of creation. The task of socialism is to make sure that man will no longer be a prey of nature, a prey of his fellow man.

QUESTION

Realistically speaking, do you think Marxism still has a chance to triumph one day?

LAYTON

Why not? If people want it. Will they want freedom? Yes.

QUESTION

But will they want to go back to Marxism after it's been so widely discredited? Or will they have to carve out a totally new ideology that hasn't been tainted by the collapse of state socialism?

LAYTON

There is no reason why Marxism should be supplanted by another philosophy. Because Marxism, as I see it, is the latest and clearest development of something that began with the Hebrew prophets and antiquity, then went on into the Renaissance, the Enlightenment, and the various social end economic movements of the nineteenth century.

QUESTION

In the sense of a humanism?

LAYTON

Absolutely. Marxism to me is the real humanism of the twentieth century. And I see no greater philosophy possible because Marxism rests on all the developments of all the social thinking, that man has done ever since he began to think seriously about society and himself.

QUESTION

So Nietzsche comes in more as a psychologist in your thinking?

LAYTON

Yes. As a wonderful psychologist. Together, Marx and Nietzsche are the great emancipators of the human intellect.

QUESTION

Marx' and Engel's critique of Christianity is very much like Nietzsche's.

LAYTON

That's why I associate Marx with Nietzsche's superman —

> I think of the young Marx,
> heaven-storming Promethean, making
> kings and capitalists quake
> with his *Grundrisse*, his black smouldering eyes
> praising unalienated man, Superman.

There I want to show that Marx and Nietzsche both want the emancipation of mankind.

QUESTION

Over recent decades you've attracted a lot of hostility for coming out in support of, say, Trudeau invoking the War Measures Act, of the American policy regarding Santo Domingo, of the American intervention in Vietnam, of Nixon's "courageous" decision to invade Cambodia, and so on and so forth.[14] Is there anything in these various statements you'd rather not have said?

LAYTON

I want to make clear that what many people thought was a perversion of my thinking came from my real fear of Soviet communism. And therefore I was wholeheartedly for America. My aim was to make sure that America was strong and would not be brought down by liberals and half-baked idealists. I wanted people to realize that the important battle was against the Soviet Union, that the Soviet Union had to be checked in its ruthless attempts to spread Soviet-style communism and that if anybody deserved credit for doing that, it would be the United States.

QUESTION

So you supported the United States but not the capitalist system.

LAYTON

I'm glad you're making that distinction. I've always opposed capitalism. I abhor it. My chief objection to capitalism is that it has meant the alienation of man from himself, his fellowman, nature and the world. That's the great sin, the great crime, and that's why I talk about unalienated man in my poem "Sunflowers." Marx saw that. Marx saw that the greatest crime and the greatest sin of capitalism was that it fosters this alienation. And I'd like to see mankind restored to its capacity for friendship and love with other human beings and with the world. And my faith still is that socialism can do that.

QUESTION

You've sketched your own nightmare vision of a future society as "run by a tolerant elite composed of scientists, well-heeled technicians, and efficient commissars buttressed by serviceable cadres of social workers and psychiatrists."[15]

LAYTON

Exactly. If we don't establish that kind of socialist humanism, that's the alternative — the Orwellian world.

QUESTION

Or Huxley's "brave new world."

LAYTON

Exactly, that's what we are faced with. Large components of that sinister scenario are already in place.

QUESTION

It's amazing to hear everyone these days praise the capitalist 'market economy' as if it were a magic formula for the salvation of mankind.

People tend to forget that this system works so well for North America, Japan, and Europe largely because it's based on the exploitation of all the rest.

LAYTON

It's just another phrase for exploitation. Naked exploitation as you observed it in Brazil. It's because the few privileged nations were able to industrialize very rapidly in the nineteenth century and into the twentieth century, which gave them a strong position *vis-à-vis* the non-industrialized world. And now they are in a position to exploit these countries and get away with it. That's where we are at now. And what I would like to see at this point is Marxism updated in a way to explain to people just what has happened, to explain to them the noble idea of an emancipation of mankind, the emancipation of the individual from anything that has trammelled him. Whatever else poetry is, it is freedom. Whatever else socialism is, it is freedom. And freedom is what man needs. Because freedom is creativity and we cannot exist without freedom. In a poem I wrote, I go so far as to say that creativity is divinity and that man is divine. This gets me very close to Blake: man is the only creative thing on this planet. That is why I always allude to Genesis where God says that He is making man in his own image. And man *has* been made in God's image. Looked at analytically, looked at closely, it means that God is creative. He is the image of creativity. And man made in God's image is creative. For me that is the essential thing about man and that is why I would fight to the end to defend him. No matter what his weaknesses are. No matter how many Hitlers he produces. Man contains the possibility of freedom because he is creative. And his creativity, I believe, will eventually allow him to make a better world than that made by his predecessors up to now.

QUESTION

Do you see any thinkers now working along these lines?

LAYTON

They don't seem to be aware of what the real issues are. That's their great weakness. They don't realize that this is the time to really get back to Marx, especially the early Marx, the Marx of the economic and philosophic manuscripts. There has never been a greater need for Marxism. My feeling is that there is more hope in the truncated

Soviet Union than there is in America. In the sense that there is a fundamental social basis and consciousness left over from their having made property public. Only they had no idea of how to administer public property and therefore it became totalitarianism. It is a terrible thing when you give the state complete power because the individual is eliminated, it's submerged, it's placed at the mercy of a monolith. It was Marx's cardinal mistake that he didn't foresee that any specific group will abuse power if it is given a monopoly on it. Well, we are wiser now. And if we do have public property we are going to make sure that it will be distributed and used democratically. And that there will be a strong democratic society. In other words, socialism without democracy cannot work. Socialism without democracy leads to tyranny and dictatorship. That's the benefit we derive from the experience of the Soviet Union. A future socialist society will have public property owned by the people. But the emphasis will be on democracy. Now the early communist theorists didn't realize just how important it was to institutionalize democracy in such a way that it could not be subverted. You can't eliminate greed.

QUESTION
You can only make use of it.

LAYTON
That's right. What we have to learn to do is make use of those things that we call evil. That's the great lesson Nietzsche taught us. He realized that greed, envy, hatred, jealousy, can all be used as energy principles. And this is also what we are learning painfully through our recent historical experiences with state socialism. But we are not going to forget these lessons. I am especially hopeful that the Soviet Union and Eastern Europe have learned from them and that when they arise from the ashes we will see a new socialism, more mature than what they started with.

NOTES

1. Irving Layton, *Taking Sides: The Collected Social and Political Writings*, ed. Howard Aster (Oakville: Mosaic Press, 1977), 162.
2. Irving Layton, *Taking Sides*, 195.

3. Elspeth Cameron, *Irving Layton: A Portrait* (Toronto: Stoddart, 1985), 58.

4. Irving Layton, *Waiting for the Messiah: A Memoir* (Toronto: McClelland and Stewart, 1985), 126.

5. Irving Layton, *Waiting for the Messiah*, 111.

6. Irving Layton is referring to Lenin's *Imperialism: The Latest Stage in the Development of Capitalism.*

7. Irving Layton is referring to Lenin's *Materialism and Emperio-criticism. Critical Comments on a Reactionary Philosophy.*

8. Irving Layton is referring to Lenin's *Left-Wing Communism: An Infantile Disorder.*

9. Cf. Trotsky's *Literature and Revolution.*

10. Irving Layton, *Waiting for the Messiah*, 117.

11. Elspeth Cameron, *Irving Layton*, 99.

12. Cf. Irving Layton, *Taking Sides*, 93; Elspeth Cameron, *Irving Layton*, 315.

13. Elspeth Cameron, *Irving Layton*, 354.

14. Cf. Irving Layton, *Taking Sides*, 101Ä2, 132–33, 151, 153–54.

15. Irving Layton, *Engagements*, ed. Seymour Mayne (Toronto: McClelland and Stewart, 1972), 93.

LAYTON AT EIGHTY:
SINGING SONGS OF LOVE

Ann Diamond

Going to interview Irving Layton, I had the feeling I was about to meet my maker. It's almost the same feeling I get when I go to see my bank manager. In both cases the question of debt arises.

If there had been no Irving Layton back in the 1960s when I was deciding what to do with my life I might have gone straight into real estate with barely a qualm. But as it happened, our country was suffering a poetry craze, the like of which has never been seen before or since. Long before I reached the age of reason, I decided to reverse the usual Anglo-Saxon order, and put 'imagination' ahead of 'survival' on my priorities list. In part, Layton is responsible for my having made this fatal mistake.

I find him at home with his fifth wife, Anna Pottier, in a happy, expansive mood. He's just been inducted into Italy's prestigious Institute Pertini, whose members include the great names in world literature and politics: Alexander Solzhenitsyn, Alexander Dubček, Saul Bellow. The news arrives as Layton is firming up plans to go to Italy in April where he will launch a bilingual edition, in English and Italian, of his book, *The Baffled Hunter*.

It turns out that Irving and I have something in common besides poetry. We both went to Baron Byng High School. He entered in the fall of 1925, and forty years later it was my turn. My suburban neighbourhood in the mid-1960s had no Protestant high school, so we commuted to Baron Byng. That's how I was first inoculated with the smells, the peculiar energy of St. Urbain Street and its displaced Mediterranean cultures: the school was then divided among Jews, Greeks and francophone Moroccans, who moved in separate, but mutually respectful worlds. To me it was exotic and a far cry from the 'burbs, and once I'd gained entry I was reluctant to come back out.

It was during Grade Eight at Baron Byng that I first heard of Irving Layton and Mordecai Richler, two writers who were helping to create a new, cosmopolitan Canadian literature. So it's strange to think of Irving Layton turning eighty on March 6. Or is it March 12?

I decide it's time to resolve the mystery surrounding Layton's birth. "When is your birthday, Irving?"

"My birthday is on the sixth of March, but Stalin died on the twelfth and since he's been my *bête noire* for a long time, I like to celebrate both at once."

Come to think of it, Layton has always celebrated things that others prefer to keep in the closet. After all, it's the poet's job and he's been at it for sixty-five years.

"The true poet is absolutely tenacious," says Layton. "He's like a sentinel. He doesn't abandon his post. He continues to speak the truth just like the prophets. That's my religion."

Certainly no one can match his singleness of purpose. Layton calls his poetic output "an all-time record." He has written sixty books, and a bibliography of his work, soon to be released, runs to 700 pages.

Are his poems really bits of divine revelation? To sit across the table from him is to entertain that possibility very seriously. To drink from his silver teapot is to catch some of his enthusiasm as he reads poems that still resonate from some ancient place of exile where a biblical harp keeps chiming and God plays an intricate chessgame with words.

Since Layton's heyday, unquestionably, love of poetry has receded in our country. In the early 1960s, poetry in Canada outsold fiction and non-fiction. People by the hundreds flocked to readings. In the 1990s, despite government funding, the audience for poetry continues shrinking. Many would say poor quality is to blame. The current cult of 'self-expression' banalizes poetry as therapy or consolation.

"At one time," Layton recalls, "there was a lot of ferment and poets were at the centre of it. Myself and Leonard Cohen and Louis Dudek and Eli Mandel from Toronto and Phyllis Webb who'd come in from Vancouver. A nice happy band of happy warriors.

"We felt we were changing things. We were bringing down the stale Victorianism that had dominated this country for over half a century. We were liberating energies, freeing the imagination. There were people who were opposed to us of course, people who felt we were treading on their orthodox toes and were furious about it."

Some of Layton's books were banned in Ontario. "I think there's no higher compliment than that," he says. The poet's job as he sees it, is always to destroy complacency and his commitment to contradiction remains immense. He fulminates, he pontificates, but he's also a passionate listener.

I bring out my Big Question. Are the Victorians back in control of Canadian poetry?

"They may be," he concedes. "But basically the poets have lost their *élan*. They're not writing the kind of work that stirs people or quickens the pulse in any way. They're not writing the kind of poetry that challenges economic and political and social and religious and sexual taboos. What they're writing I call kitchen-sink poetry, and it springs from the fact that people are so frightened about the future and about the present, they're so uncertain about themselves, that they can't think deeply and freshly about the problems confronting them."

He names exceptions: David Solway, Anne Cimon, Michael Harris. But he sees contemporary poetry taking the place of organized religion as a provider of comfort and reassurance. "Real poetry, like true religion, does the opposite. It tells people that precisely because you're suffering and in turmoil, that's good. It means you're not dead."

The interview has ended, or at least the tape has run out. We rewind it so Irving can hear how he sounds these days. With obvious delight, he listens to his own voice describing the Grade Six teacher, Miss Benjamin, who inspired his first poem. He lingers on details, her tight blouse and lush breasts, which inspired his twelve-year-old lust. If I were an unmitigated Puritan, like some of his critics, I suppose I might attack him for this, but who can deny that it's touching and true?

Afterwards he beams, "I believe I have to be the last love poet anywhere. Love has always been the very foundation of my work."

"Don't forget rage," I remind him.

"Love and rage and — sex. What else is there?" To prove his point, he launched *Dance With Desire*, his collected love poems, at Magnum Bookstore in Ottawa on International Women's Day.

This coincidence of dates brings us to the thorny issue of Layton's record in relationships, a sore point with feminists. I ask him point blank if he's a serial monogamist.

"Yes," he says, "but I have yet to be convicted."

"And I'm his latest victim," Anna chimes in, smiling radiantly.

Says Layton in self-defence, "I like to leave them happy, rather than dead."

In Canada, the verdict still isn't in on Irving Layton, and some would say there isn't a jury in the country that could give him a fair trial. Attempts to put him in his place or 'expose' him all stumble against the reality of his achievement. Elspeth Cameron's notorious portrait did much to prove that there is still little room in our country for a poet of his range and stature.

You can accuse a poet of the most heinous crimes and personal failings without doing the slightest damage to his reputation. Perhaps some day Canada's army of critic/moralists will realize that they've missed the twentieth century. We don't need poets to live exemplary, much less conventional, lives. We need them to write great poems. Irving Layton has kept his side of the bargain.

When I finally leave, I have the impression that I've been taken in again — duped into believing in poetry by someone who calls himself Irving Layton.

And the funny thing is, I'm grateful.

Irving Layton, F.R. Scott, and Louis Dudek at reunion
and launching for *CIV/n: A Literary Magazine of the 50s*
(edited by Aileen Collins), 5 March 1983.
Photo: Tim Clark. Courtesy of Véhicule Press.

LOVE AND LOATHING: THE ROLE OF WOMAN IN IRVING LAYTON'S VISION

Veneranda Kreipans-McGrath

LOVE AND IMAGINATION: REDEMPTIVE POSSIBILITIES

"How to dominate reality? Love is one way;
imagination another . . ."
— "The Fertile Muck," *The Bull Calf,* 1956

Layton's poetry from his earliest work to his latest book of poems, *For My Neighbors in Hell* (1979), manifests a consistent concern with the inherent tension between the creative and the destructive forces of life and death, or as he claims in his foreword to *The Tightrope Dancer* (1978), "sex and death." The problem for the poet or the artist is to learn how to live "poised on a rope stretched tautly between sex and death." Reflecting on the human condition and the nature of man, Layton adds;

> Perhaps the poets's tightrope is not stretched between sexuality and death, but between love and loathing for the human race.

The imagery in the poem "The Tightrope Dancer" (*The Tightrope Dancer*) vividly presents the basic tension between the antagonistic forces of creativity and destruction in life and in man in the lines, "Awareness of death's pull / into nothingness," contrasted with ". . . the prod, the harsh shove of love. . . ." The important theme which emerges in this poem is Layton's consistent affirmation of sexual love, as a creative force which opposes the destructive forces in life.

Layton's concern is not only with the process of natural death manifested in the cyclical pattern of nature — life, death, and rebirth — but also with death as a form of death-in-life. His poem "Late Invitation to the Dance" (*The Tightrope Dancer*) presents the dialectical tension between the antagonistic forces in the symbolic image of the fragile butterfly contrasted with the images of death and destruction:

> [My] disenchantment with the human race that has hardened like cement or settled like a freshly dug grave over which hovers a single butterfly.

The poet's disenchantment is presented through images of death, destruction and alienation:

> Revolutions, wars, assassinations, and the deaths of great and famous men — all the familiar troubles. And explorations into space to find God wandering among the galaxies and to bring him back to his creatures dying of loneliness and anomie.

Nevertheless, the poet's attitude to life remains one of celebration and affirmation of the creative principle in life. He concludes:

> Under the white stars I carry in my headpiece the same unshakable faith in the holiness of reason, beauty, and love.

Layton's poetry affirms that the Dionysian man, or the creative artist, must "dance" upon the tightrope between two antagonistic realities. Man and artist must commute between the two realities: his "everyday reality"[1] (the awareness of the tragedy of man's human condition and his destructive civilization as illustrated in "Late Invitation to the Dance") and the "Dionysian reality"[2] (the realm of man's artistic imagination, the powers of illusion through art, and the process of transformation through sensual love). Through the power of sensual love and the power of art, man is able to transcend the limits of his ordinary world. Through the process of transformation in love and art, man is able to redefine his reality to give it form and meaning. Wynne Francis in "Layton and Nietzsche" states:

> The most powerful life is the creative life . . . The human Dionysian poet is therefore both the creation and the analogue of the divine artist, since he recreates himself and the world in every poem he writes.[3]

Layton resembles the "human Dionysian poet" in that his poetry consistently affirms the sensual life of the body as a source of redemption and inspiration to man. In his poem "Signs and Portents" (*Lovers and Lesser Men*, 1973) he says: "It has taken me all these years to discover that everything except / writing poems and making love ends up by finally boring me."

The theme of celebration and affirmation of the Dionysian elements in life is contained in the poem "Logos" (*Collected Poems*, 1965), one of Layton's strongest images of life celebration:

> I laugh and praise the Dionysian
> Everywhere irrational thrust
> That sends meteors spilling into dust,
> This enchantment risen in the bone.

A poem, intense in tone and imagery which celebrates the creative life and extends the affirmation through the dance image is "For Mao Tse-Tung: A Meditation on Flies and Kings" (*A Laughter in the Mind*, 1959).

> How to dominate reality? Love is one way,
>   imagination another. Sit here
> beside me, sweet; take my hard hand in yours.
>   We'll mark the butterflies disappearing over the hedge
> with tiny wristwatches on their wings:
> our fingers touching the earth, like two Buddhas.
>   "The Fertile Muck" (*The Bull Calf*, 1956)

In these lines Layton presents a profound and striking image which symbolically illustrates the Dionysian state: man and woman in unity of sensual love. The poet affirms their unity with microcosm and with the macrocosm, in full acceptance of the cycle of life, the natural process of life, death and rebirth. The "butterflies," love and imagination, are wearing "wristwatches" which indicate that they are also caught in the Cosmic order and process of nature — time: life, death, and rebirth. The universe is in a constant process of change and flux which includes all creation. The poem also manifests the paradox in the inherent unity in the tension of the opposing forces of life and death.

The important theme which emerges in "The Fertile Muck" is the poet's observation that love and art not only transform or "dominate" man's reality, but that *only* through love and art (imagination) is man able to transcend himself. The essential aim for man or artist is to fulfil himself as a human being and to achieve a sense of unity with the Cosmos outside. In the image of the "two Buddhas" with "our fingers touching the earth," Layton affirms the redemptive function of love and art in man's life.

The poet also notes that the inherent tension between the creative and destructive forces of life and death, or sex and death, creates a "tightrope" upon which man and artist must learn to "dance" or define himself. Man and artist, cast against the destructive forces of dissolution and death-in-life, is able to assert his individuality and define himself in a creative life through the redemptive powers of love and art.

THE FEMALE PRINCIPLE: WOMAN AS INTERMEDIARY

1. *Woman as The Other*

Women and poems are my sole chance here to give
expelled breath shape and contour and fable it
with meaning.

"The Tamed Puma"

In several poems such as "The Tamed Puma" (*The Poems of Irving Layton*, 1977) Layton confirms the importance that woman holds in man's life. She is the Other through whom man defines himself, who gives scope and meaning to his life. In his foreword to *The Love Poems of Irving Layton* (1980) he states:

So I take my place beside the poets, and less arrogant than the philosopher or mystic, am prepared to find the greatest good and embrace God whenever I hold a woman in the act of love. It is then I know with assurance and inexpressible delight that whatever it is life promises us, this must be it; and that a universe containing this experience must have something grandly important going for it.

Woman is intrinsically connected to life. She is the generative principle responsible for man's biological and erotic life (rebirth into manhood). She is also a source of his spiritual life in that through the experience of woman in sensual love, man is able to transcend, and fulfil himself as a human being.

As Simone de Beauvoir states, "Man seeks in woman the Other as Nature and as his fellow being."[4] The other as Nature (woman) can be seen in the ancient symbol of the goddess Isis, the essence of woman intrinsically connected to life.

The redemptive and inspirational power of the goddess Isis, of woman as the creative source of life, is manifested in Layton's poem "The Convert" (*Droppings from Heaven*, 1978):

> Just when my faith is strongest
> and I embrace Emptiness
>
> . . . .
>
> just then he turns his head
> to smile goodness and peace at me
> with your full perfect lips
> and at that instant
> I fall down on my knees
> an awestruck convert,
> my eyes two candles glimmering
> in the dark

Man feels alone and alienated; he has an overwhelming sense of "Emptiness" within and around him. It is only through the Other, as a part of Nature, that his faith in Nature is restored. These lines illustrate the redemptive power of woman; however, redemption comes first through sensual love. Through love, woman proceeds to inspire a renewal of faith in man, a renewal of his belief in life. The imagery in the poem — "my eyes two candles glimmering / in the dark" — symbolically represents the rebirth of faith. Now, although the emptiness around him is still vast, the light of the reborn spirit is alive and it illuminates the darkness.

Thus, woman as the Other, and as a part of Nature, serves man as a source of redemption from his loneliness and alienation in the Cosmos. She acts as an intermediary between man and God.

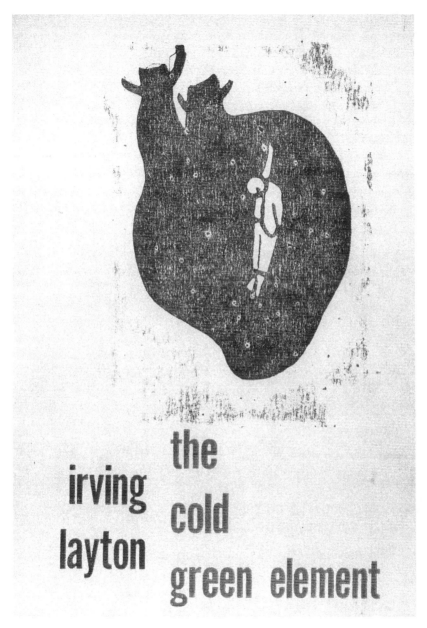

Cover of Irving Layton's *The Cold Green Element* published in 1955 by Contact Press. The cover was designed by Betty Sutherland.

11. *Woman In Man's World*

Woman I loved. Enough
She made me dream of love
And in that sexual dream
   forget the whitethroat's scream.
                     "Orpheus" (*The Cold Green Element*, 1955)

The role of woman as a source of redemption and inspiration also applies to the concrete world of men. She stands as the Other to whom man may turn for refuge against the horrors of man-made history. Simone de Beauvoir explains the *passive* and *dependent* role of woman in history:

> History has shown us that men have always kept in their hands all concrete powers; since the earliest days of the patriarchate they have thought best to keep woman in a state of dependence; their codes of law have been set against her; and thus she has been definitely established as the Other.[5]

Layton's attitude to woman in relation to man's control of "the concrete powers" is precisely that defined by Simone de Beauvoir. As the Other, woman has the power to offer redemption and salvation to man from the horror of his history. Her role nevertheless remains a *passive* one. It is man who must *actively* choose his salvation. The *dependent* aspect of woman upon man reveals itself in the fact that man, in choosing salvation for himself, saves both man and woman. In the poem, "He Saw Them At First" (*The Shattered Plinths*, 1968), the poet clearly illustrates woman's *passive* position in a man's "concrete" world, her *dependence* upon his action, and her role as a source of salvation:

> He approached and saw one that appeared to be female
> and drew her out of the circle of excrement-covered
> figures, catching and holding her reeking arm
> in its half-movement of violence
>   "He Saw Them At First"

Layton presents the state of man's history as a vision of hell, destruction, violence and madness. Woman too, "her reeking arm / in its half-movement of violence," has become a victim and an accomplice to man's madness. Nevertheless, as she is the source of life, she can never really turn against life, and therefore redemption can still be found in woman. The poem implies that since it is the history of man's control of "concrete powers" (active role) which is the source of destruction, it is therefore man himself who must decide to put a stop to the destruction. Man must choose life over death as salvation for both. However, although woman retains her passive role as a source of redemption and inspiration, in the realm of love she may assume an active role *to inspire love*. The poet says, ". . . she threw herself on him / and cried joyously: 'I love you.' Without looking up / he muttered to the crackling sand, 'And I, you.' " D.H. Lawrence in *Fantasia of the Unconscious* states:

> If the man, as thinker and doer, is active . . . The man may be the initiator in action, but the woman is initiator in emotion.[6]

Layton's attitude to the role of woman clearly indicates a similar perception. In the realm of emotion woman may assume the active role of initiating or inspiring love, but in the world of "concrete powers," it is man who remains in the active role.

III. *Woman and Man in Nature*

One of the central concepts in Layton's poetry is the patriarchal conviction that woman was created by God for man. Man holds the primary position in existence, woman the secondary. As Simone de Beauvoir explains, "Woman thus seems to be the inessential who never goes back to being the essential, to be the absolute Other, without reciprocity."[7] De Beauvoir further illustrates the strength of this patriarchal conviction in *everyman*:

> This conviction is dear to the male, and every creation myth has expressed it, among others the legend of Genesis.

According to the patriarchal view, woman exists not as an end in herself but in order to serve as a companion to man (Adam), and to rescue him from loneliness and alienation:

> Eve was not fashioned at the same time as the man; she was not fabricated from a different substance, nor of the same clay as

was used to model Adam: she was taken from the flank of the first male. Not even her birth was independent; God did not spontaneously choose to create her as an end in herself . . . She was destined by Him for man; it was to rescue Adam from loneliness that He gave her to him, in her mate was her origin and purpose.[8]

Layton's poem "Adam" (*For My Brother Jesus*, 1976) begins "I wish we could go back / to the beginning / " where "There's only God and myself / in the cool first evening." The imagery in the poem suggests a calm, serene setting. God and man are in unity, "discussing his fantastic creation," observing the beauty and magnificence of the universe, "the moon and the stars, / and the enveloping stillness." However, man *is* alone and solitary. God tells him about woman, the creation which He specifically designed for man. The woman (Eve) to be created, has not yet appeared; therefore the setting is very calm. However, the final lines of the poem: "we talk softly for a long time / and very very carefully," express a sense of foreboding about the nature of the second creation.

In "La Minerve" (*The Love Poems of Irving Layton*, 1980) the poet expresses man's first delight in his vision of the new creation. Adam sees Eve for the first time and realizes that this magnificent creation is made for him:

> But when you stand at night before me
> Like the genius of this place, naked,
> All my ribs most unpaganlike ache
> With foolstruck Adam in his first wonder.

Here is the patriarchal conviction that God created Eve from one of Adam's ribs: woman is the Other, a secondary creation. The very purpose of her existence is to bring joy and salvation to man.

In his poem, "Return to Eden" (*The Tightrope Dancer*, 1978), the poet once again says, "You were sent to me," implying that woman came to him in order to save him from loneliness and to offer him salvation in the form of sensual love:

> so that I could make my declaration of love
> beside a royal palm

and afterwards kiss your small ears
under the chorisia's white floss.

Another poem, "Orthodoxy" (*Droppings from Heaven*, 1979)
expresses the poet's gratitude to God for the marvellous creation,
woman:

And he is all-merciful
for how barren would be my days
were you not mine
to delight and amaze

The central themes which emerge from these poems depict woman
as the Other who acts as an intermediary between man and Nature,
and man and God. She is a part of Nature. In her generative capacity
woman becomes intrinsically connected to life. She is the source of
natural life and erotic life in man. Thus, in her very existence woman
asserts life and serves as a source of redemption and salvation to man
from his loneliness, his alienation, and the horrors of his man-made
world. She is the necessary Other through whom man may fulfil
himself and give scope and meaning to his life.

ARCHETYPAL FEMININE: THE MYTH OF WOMAN

IV. *The Great Goddess: Eve-Circe*

Layton's poetry concerning woman in the Edenic realm is lyrical and
rich in evocative imagery. The sun, representing the creative love
principle, Eros, (the dominant symbol in his love poetry) is a
"blazing Greek sun" ("Vexata Quaestio," *The Collected Poems*, 1965)
emitting the creative energy of life. The night is seen as soft and
sensual as "In the purpling dusk I softly call your name / . . . Soon
the ballerina stars will come dancing out," ("Of The Man Who Sits
In The Garden," *For My Brother Jesus*, 1976). Darkness and light fuse
into creative unity wherein the essence of each element is strength-
ened by the contrast of the other. Symbolically, man and woman in
their very difference affirm each other's essence. The poem, "For
Francesca" (*For My Brother Jesus*) illustrates the poet's lyrical use of

imagery, music, darkness and light, to create the sensual mood of the Edenic realm:

> . . . ignite each other
> into a flame
> that lights my room's darkness
> till I think the night has gone
>
> The dawn comes
> when I open my window
> to let music and flame
> astonish the whole world.

In his poem, "Earth Goddess" (*The Bull Calf*) dedicated to Marilyn Monroe, Layton addresses her as a "goddess," invoking her to use her creative power to redeem man:

> Teach us happiness,
> The warmth, love, sanity
> Of your redeeming energy:
> Blest of women, earth goddess,
> Teach us to delight and praise.

The image of Venus/Aphrodite rising naked from the foam of the sea is a recurrent image in Layton's love poetry. In the poem, "Proteus and Nymph" (*The Love Poems of Irving Layton*), he imagines woman transformed into a goddess of erotic love. Through his experience of women in sensual love, he sees woman like the goddess Aphrodite rising from the waves to save and delight man:

> . . . I'm thinking of the waves
>   gently cupping the breasts
> of the lovely nymph just risen from the sea
>   and the water lapping
> her thighs and her delicate love-cleft
>
> When she swims away
>   she pulls my thoughts after her
> in watery streaks of light. I become
>   the sea around her . . .

Man himself becomes transformed by the overpowering beauty and grace of the goddess or sea nymph. In his imagination the poet assumes the essence of the sea water around the nymph which is caressing her beautiful body:

> and she nestles in my long green arms
> or is held in the flowing
> wavelets of my white hair. I billow
> above her like a dolphin
> stroke her limbs and nip her rosy neck and shoulders
> with sharp unceasing kisses
> till languorously she slips to the ribbed sand
> where under the haloing starfish
> fern weed and enamoured seasnake I quiver
> between her silver thighs

The imagery of the poem suggests the soft, sensual fluid movement of sea, water representing the grace of movement of woman in her passive, receptive form to man. However, man himself is seduced by the irresistible charms of the sea nymph as he surrenders himself to her in love.

In poems such as "Prelude" (*The Shattered Plinths*) or "Undine" (*The Bull Calf*) the poet perceives woman as a siren, a sea nymph, a Venus/Aphrodite rising out of the sea. The poet's vision of the archetypal myth of the birth of Venus seems to be a re-enacting of the ancient myth of Adam and Eve. In a different form, the poet repeats the ancient legend of creation over and over again in the image of the birth of Venus, Aphrodite, or Eve. The central theme in such poems is the poet's conscious (artistic) and unconscious (archetypal) affirmation of woman as a creation by God for man's redemption and inspiration.

The poet associates his experience of love for women with the myth of the sea nymph who lures man, her lover Paracelsus, to the depths of the sea, representing the profound and complex experience of love. He reveals the sexual power of the 'goddess' (woman) in that his desire for her love is so profound that he feels totally possessed by it. The poem also manifests the dark side of the power of the 'goddess' in that man feels completely in her power: "Fish a soul for you from between my loins; / You shudder in my embrace / And all your wetness takes the form of tears." The sense of loss of self under the power of love, and the sense of sorrow in the image of water as tears, reveal the disturbing power of Eros. Love demands total surrender from man for the gift of the gods. The gift consists of ecstatic *moments* of transformation and transcendence into the realm of the gods.

The complexity of the figure of woman as explored and manifested in myth or archetype is explained by Eric Neumann:

> This wreath of symbolic images, however, surrounds not only one figure, but a great number of figures, of Great Mother who, as goddesses and fairies, female demons and nymphs, friendly and unfriendly, manifest the one Great Unknown, the Great Mother as the central aspect of the Archetypal Feminine, in the rites and myths, the religions and legends of mankind.[9]

The tension between man's surrender of self in love and his fight for identity is expressed in his myth of a dark version of Eve, the 'goddess' Circe. Woman's destructive power evokes hatred and anger in man which he manifests in the creation of a negative, destructive, dangerous 'goddess' (woman) Circe.

The imagery in Layton's poetry concerning woman as Circe is dark and sombre. *Wind*, representing her fickle changing nature, her instability ("unstable as the wind") in "Woman" (*The Bull Calf*) and *rain*, (negative image of water), are the dominant images which create a mood of unrest, depression, conflict, and anger. Man is in conflict with himself and with woman. Therefore, man is in conflict with nature.

The poem "Rain" (*A Laughter in the Mind*, 1959) begins with the lines, "The wind blew hard in the trees / And palegreen was the wet grass." The green colour is a pale, sick green. The wind and storm set a mood of unrest, anger and depression. The lover (woman) is false to him, and deceitful as she says, "I love you, Love . . . / And gave her false mouth to kiss." The story and atmosphere in the poem suggest the setting of the old ballads wherein the actual drama of a murder of a loved one is acted out. In this poem, the poet also murders his false love, "I lay down her bleeding corpse." The vivid images become quite gory as "The rain fell" and the murdered lover decomposes and becomes part of the earth which receives her, "how green the moss!" The lover is absolved of his crime by "the white rain," as it cleans his hands of her blood and his guilt. The treacherous, deceitful woman deserves to die because her crime is greater than his: death is a just penalty for a deceitful lover. In the poem, the poet has created a fantasy wherein he actually kills the false lover. Even in her negative form, woman evokes strong emotion from man — hatred, which is the other side of love. And even through her negative and destructive image, woman is able to inspire man to experience life in its full intensity of creation and destruction. Through woman, he realizes the profound depths of his own darkness. Thus, even in her negative form woman remains a mirror of man's own complexity, and an inspiration to explore and express his complexity as a human being.

In "Fanatic in San Feliu" (*The Love Poems of Irving Layton*), Layton creates a powerful image of Eden (post-lapsarian) in its destructive form, wherein Circe reigns supreme. The lines, "They said it wouldn't rain / after the 21st of June / in San Feliu," symbolically suggests the poet's disappointment that the enchanted garden of Eden has a dark element: "It did, / It rained every day." The poet becomes aware that the post-lapsarian Eden is an enchanted garden wherein both Eve and Circe reign in equal power. And Eros manifests the nature of love in its dual aspect, creative and destructive. Layton's vision of the garden of Eden is not ideal, or static. It is characterized by turbulence and transience. Thus, the negative image of the "rainswept" garden of Eden reflects the poet's torment and his "terrible sickness" (love):

> Now under this soaked awning
> beside an abandoned aquarium
> full of crawling baby lobsters
> whose rubbery black eyes
> I imagine moles
> on your lifeless breasts
> are only some empty chairs
> and myself,
> a lonely fanatic with images
> of your faraway body
> and corrupt mouth
> to torment him this rainswept

cold evening
while the high and swelling wind
howls with his terrible sickness.

Instead of a sky with a moon and stars (representing the positive image of the garden of Eden), the poet is caught under a "soaked awning," with an "aquarium" instead of the vast magnificence of the sea. There is no Undine or sea nymph, but only "baby lobsters" with "rubbery black eyes." Once again, the poet fantasizes the death of his deceitful love. He is alone and abandoned, suffering the torture of his "terrible sickness," his love for woman who has left him.

In these strong negative images, the poet reflects the bleakness and desolation within a man's soul when he has been abandoned by a woman he loves. However, at the same time, the very intensity of the pain of love suggests its positive aspect which is the profundity of the love that man is able to feel for woman.

The important fact which emerges from the study of the negative images of woman as Circe, is that the poems never reflect the destructive power of Circe as a form of life-in-death, but rather confirm destruction and the negative aspect of woman as the necessary polarity to creation. As Simone de Beauvoir says:

> There is no figurative image of woman which does not call up at once its opposite: she is Life and Death, Nature and Artifice, Daylight and Night . . . In the figures of the Virgin Mary and Beatrice, Eve and Circe still exist.[10]

Woman is life, and as life she reflects in her very essence the duality of Nature. In the figure of woman, man is constantly aware of the tension between Life and Death, and between the creative and destructive principles of life, Eros and Thanatos. The awareness of the basic principle of life, the paradox of the unity of the constant tension between the creative and destructive forces of life, compels man to accept his own duality. Thus, man is able to fulfil himself as a human being by his active choice to define himself in a creative life. Woman, in the complex structure of her essence, allows man to explore the profound depths of his own nature.

NOTES

1. F. Nietzsche, *The Birth of Tragedy and The Case of Wagner*. Trans. with commentary by Walter Kaufman. (New York: Vintage Press, 1967), 59.

2. Ibid, 59.

3. Wynne Francis, "Layton and Nietzsche," *Canadian Literature*, no. 67 (Winter, 1976): 39–32.

4. Simone de Beauvoir, *The Second Sex*. (New York: Knopf, 1953), 133.

5. Ibid, 129.

6. D.H. Lawrence, *Fantasia of the Unconscious, Pyschoanalysis and the Unconscious*. (Markham, Ont.: Penguin, 1971), 98.

7. Simone de Beauvoir, *The Second Sex*. (New York: Knopf, 1953), 131.

8. Ibid, 131.

9. Erich Neumann, *The Great Mother: An Analysis of the Archetype*. Trans. Ralph Manheim. (Princeton: Princeton, 1963), 307.

10. Simone de Beauvoir, *The Second Sex*. (New York: Knopf, 1953), 131.

[Excerpts from M.A. thesis in English, Concordia University, 1980.]

A PUGNACIOUS LOVE

William Goodwin

And into all things from her Air inspired
the spirit of love and amorous delight.
— *Milton*

CRETE IN MID-SUMMER AUGUST 1965

I

To visit the grave of Nikos Kazantsakis in Crete's prefecture of Heraklion, we ascended the wooden staircase of a broad earthen mound where a huge cross of heavy brown logs stood in its centre, stripped of any inscription whatsoever. Bare in its isolation, the residing spirit seemed to call for some memorial. Seated at the foot of the cross with some sweet Demos wine for libation, we regaled ourselves with laudatory remarks and toasts to the rebellious author of "The Last Temptation of Christ," and of "Zorba," both of which celebrate sexuality and pay homage to women. The modern Dionysian let it be known that the greatest sin for a man to commit is to refuse a woman's sexual requests. We began to drink and dance slowly, with ever increasing merriment and bravado blinding us to the presence of Greek juveniles who had silently observed us from a distance. When they approached, being unable to address them in their own language, Irving took a few coins from his pocket and was utterly taken aback by their adamant refusal. They smiled and shook their heads in disapproval. To memorialize this encounter I saw him the next day at the jewellers preparing to place two drachmas in a metallic diptych — one as touchstone to the heart's corruptibility, the other as its talisman.

Was he reminded of his earlier experiences working in a children's orphanage; or was he tapped into his own struggles with poverty during the severe depression of the early 1930s when a similar refusal would be just as bizarre? How can we square Irving's equation? On one side we have just witnessed a ritual celebration of a gargantuan pleasure in life's feast, followed by bitter irony nurtured in man's follies, demonstrating the involutional insanity of history with his own Jewish tribal consciousness at its seminal core. We can readily find a great deal of evidence of this innate pessimism, a profound sense of evil, in his work. A few examples will suffice. In "No Wild Dog" he writes:

> I tell my class
> What man can do
> No Cobra Can
> And no wild Dog
>
> Or other kind
> Of vicious beast
> The prowling wolf
> And the mongoose.

Again in "Like a Mother Demented:"

> as horrorstruck we find our condemned selves on the stage
> beside her, nature's most murderous tool and accomplice.

Layton would achieve a syncretism of these powerful opposing emotions in his poetry; what he thought ultimately about its efficacy is also revealed in the following lines he had written much earlier:

> I tell you, William,
> there isn't a ghost
> of a chance
> people will be changed by poems.
> > "For My Friend Who Teaches Literature"

11

Before leaving mainland Greece for Crete we had spent the night in a comfortable room in Piraeus. It was sultry and we sat on the edge of our beds, talking past midnight about Irving's recent marriage break-up with Betty Sutherland. By this time I was already familiar with the crushing aspects of the conflict, but did not fully understand the pain or grief he felt over a situation he was unable to control. He was hurting as he attacked his vacillation, excoriated his moral lapses and took full blame for his failed marriage in expressions of guilt and remorse.

What was memorable for me this night was the sadness in the sighs and hesitation of his quiet voice carrying his conviction in what he was saying about his failed marriage — a mood I had never observed before, except in his poetry, and which was presently upstaging his usual enthusiasm and ardour. In such lines as these for Betty, he confessed:

> I would for your sake be gentle
> Be, believe me, other than I am:
> What, what madness is it that hurls me
> Sundays against your Sunday calm?
> . . .
> I swear I'm damned to so hate and rage.
> But your fair innocence is my guilt.
>
> from "I Would for Your Sake be Gentle"

In a "Letter to a Lost Love," a poem that could have been addressed to another ladylove, he also expressed a profound despair:

> But in the here and now I have a misery
> to last my life and if I don't tear a hole
> in my heart as wide and deep as its pain
> it's because I've Byron's way of seeing things
> And think death even more absurd than life
> and once dead there's no more laughing then.

Again in "My Flesh Comfortless" he writes:

> O, Love, enclose me in your round bead
>
> O lift me like a vine-leaf on the vine;
> In community of soil and sun
> Let me not taste this desolation.

One can understand his character if we balance his natural aggressiveness, or pugnacity if you will, with his reputation as a lover. His acting is superb and he projects the image of the Nietzschean superman, but one realizes too that he is very sensitive, compassionate, and free-spirited, subject to real despair, guilt and remorse, as anyone familiar with his work will allow. Not unlike the much admired biblical David, he fought the "Philistines" and took "Bathsheba," who would finally ask for absolution from the sought-after messiah, in adultery. This image best describes him for me: a star, undiminished at eighty, focused on this brutal faithless century, who continues to shine with his pugnacious human love.

III

To continue with our travels. Since no means of transportation existed beyond Knossos, we set out on foot, relying on the help of carters laden with fruit and vegetables to reach the southern tip of the island. We arrived in the dark, fatigued from traversing an empty plain halfway disappearing into high mountain ridges, where winding passes made travelling at night especially dangerous. In the folds of darkness we heard the murmur of lapping waves and descried a grotto-like edifice covered with a matting of rushes or thin animal hairs, looking most strange and challenging. To our surprise we entered freely into a fairly lit, smokey room with a polished stone-flagged floor and came face to face with a room full of wild corybantic excitement in dance and music.

Once seated at table and immediately served our dinner we were informed by the inn's unapologetic proprietor that since no sleeping quarters were available we would have to sleep on the floor. We did not object.

We had not yet finished our meal when we were suddenly approached by two young American students. Obviously alarmed by the effects of their blandishments on their Greek suitors, they vehemently requested Irving to accompany them without delay to Heraklion. Without considering the hardship and danger of night travel, nor the women's insobriety, he unhesitatingly assented, for he enjoyed the role of saviour; nor were we surprised when the car passed through a cordon of irate votaries. Yet worse was to follow, for we were embarking on a nightmare with a drunken driver and were about to careen to our deaths on a dimly lit mountain road in the grip of an alien moon's enchantment. However, all our rueful misgivings suddenly ended in an abrupt stop at the edge of the highway, one wheel teetering over a cliff. Fortunately this had a sobering effect on everyone, especially the driver, and we were able to complete the journey in tranquillity, grateful to be alive and well as we arrived in Heraklion at 3:00 a.m. But, this was not the end.

Later there was a need for some explanation, for this brush with death was almost a metaphysical one: being an anomaly recognized by Freud as the death wish, or the antinomy to Layton's gargantuan vitality. Could it be explained as the sedulous pursuit of the existential moment — to experience the maximum awareness of danger, perhaps see the true visage of death, the ultimate reality that defines life as well as art, love and religion, the Absolute that enriches all our salutary presumptions? To these ruminations Layton smilingly, fraternally, replied by placing his arm on my shoulder and gently completing this gesture with a terse breezy "Death! Shmeth! A guardian angel, my venerable mother, protected me, as she always has."

Like former Prime Minister of Canada, Mackenzie King, Layton had in early infancy formed a mystical relation to his mother who, he explains, nurtured his poetic processes and protected him from dire evil:

> O fierce she was, mean and unaccommodating;
> But I think now of the toss of her gold earrings,
> Their proud carnal assertion, and her youngest sings
> While all the rivers of her red veins move into the sea.
>   "Keine Lazarovitch 1870–1959"

This relation, a spiritual hermaphroditism, was always inherent in the women with whom he had intimate contact. Hence there was more than a physical relation that he celebrated in his so-called sex poems. Again, whatever symbiosis he achieved, it was through his poetry; as such, women were his life-blood. He loved women for they were his second nature, his "rib," the better part, more sensitive and compassionate self, open to their intimate life-styles and stories, their swinging moods ("Swinging Flesh"), beauty, love-inspiring faculties; lifting man, the stubborn Adam, out of the rut he enjoyed. What a wonderful antidote to rationality, mechanism and statism!

I hope that this account of our Cretan peregrinations bore fruit in other respects, as an attempt to reveal another facet of Layton's complex character normally hidden from the public eye.

IRVING LAYTON:
A PORTRAIT (BY A DIFFERENT
BARRIE NATIVE)

Joyce Dawe Friedman

To reflect on a friendship of thirty years and come up with a single anecdote is difficult. Even as I speak, I can barely suppress my pleasure in knowing Irving Layton.

We've all had hard and terrible times in our lives. My youth was spent just outside of Barrie, Ontario, in a rural community that was totally WASP. Need I say more! I was doomed when I reached the age of reason. Twenty years of admonitions, recriminations and denouncements, stifled any remnants of childhood laughter.

Meeting Irving through a newspaper article saved my life. Moreover, I was able to deliver my children from the land of No-No. They are all, every one of them, thoughtful, intelligent, and imaginative human beings. Their laughter resounds all over this continent.

Living in the United States, I am well aware that Canada has a better quality of life for its citizens. There's no Irving Layton here, the last freedom is commercial, and writers have long ago been put to sleep. Saul Bellow is on the "Committee for Social Thought," Gore Vidal is manipulated by the media, and Norman Mailer is normal. The great poets are gone, the new ones are in books, and the country is illiterate. Women, far behind their Canadian counterparts, are finally finding a voice, but it is late.

Irving Layton is far more than a writer. He's created a country that gives freedom a foothold and the majority an artistic landscape, whether or not they appreciate it, deserve it or choose to ignore it. He's not only a writer, he's a spokesman for truth and justice forever. He's made Canadians collectively far more than they are individually, though he champions the individual always. Most of all, he's a great artist in the true sense. His deeds are equal to his words.

With his laughter and love of life so contagious, I don't know whether the French *joie de vivre* created Irving Layton, or whether he created *joie de vivre*. Either way, he's a godsend.

AN UNLIKELY FRIENDSHIP

Dorothy Rath

On the night of March 21, 1963, a roomful of people waited in the London Public Library. They had come to hear and see poet Irving Layton who had just received the Governor-General's Award for his book, *A Red Carpet for the Sun*.

In the audience were several members of the London Poetry Workshop Group, some of whom had gone to hear Layton read earlier at York University in Toronto. They had returned fired with inspiration, their subsequent poems showing a freer, livelier style than before. "He's coming to read here in London," they had told me excitedly. "You simply MUST go to hear him — he's marvelous!" So here I sat, compliant and a bit bored. Never having read any of his work, controversial or otherwise — in fact, having only recently heard of him from my fellow poets — I didn't know what to expect. When this short, powerful figure with shaggy black hair and eyebrows came hurrying toward the platform, I exclaimed: "My God — it's Mr. Hyde!" and was promptly shushed for my irreverence. "But Spencer Tracy is my favourite actor," I protested.

As he began to read in his electrifying voice — "Keine Lazarovitch," "The Bull Calf," "The Birth of Tragedy," "The Fertile Muck," and many more — I became convinced that those piercing eyes were looking directly at me, drawn by my own intense gaze.

After the reading I joined the group of autograph seekers, feeling a tremendous need to be seen by this vibrant man as a kindred soul, an individual worthy of his notice. When my turn came I asked Mr. Layton to include my name with his signature, in the vain hope that he might recognize it later when two of my poems were to be printed in *Fiddlehead Magazine*. When I eagerly searched his book the following morning his voice still echoed in my ears, making the poems come alive again on the page. Ignoring my housework I began to compose a glowing tribute to him — free verse, of course!

I mailed it to him and was thrilled to receive a generous note in reply, complimenting me on my honesty and "very fine free verse rhythm." Encouraged, I continued to write to him, out of my need to communicate with someone in the World of Ideas, and specifically, with him! His letters to me were less frequent, of course, due as much to his many commitments as to his ambivalent feelings and personal problems. Much later he told me that I had used *love* and *imagination* effectively to *dominate reality* — that emotional demands like mine were made on him by many people, but that few of them had my depth and warmth.

I started to include amusing greeting cards, cartoons and newspaper or magazine articles of interest to him. During his sabbaticals in Europe he often wrote to thank me for keeping him informed: "You're my one and only dependable lifeline to the world," he wrote from Tel Aviv . . . "What would I do without your wonderful letters, so full of news about me and thee?. . . Those welcome snippets of info help me to keep my vanity in a good state of health." A few years after meeting him I moved to Toronto with my family. When Irving wrote that he was also moving there to teach at York University he said: "Think of it — I shan't be a stranger passing through but a Torontonian like yourself. Two Torontonians with a single thought — how to make life in Toronto endurable! To Murray's we will go. To Murray's we will go."

We met often after that for coffee or wine and cheese. He listened indulgently and with apparent interest to my accounts of life as I experienced it and I, in turn, listened patiently when he pontificated or railed against stupidity or narrow-mindedness. He became used to seeing my face in the audience at most of his readings in and around the city. One summer, however, when my husband and I were holidaying in Banff, we saw an announcement that Irving was to give a reading at the Banff Centre's Margaret Greenham Theatre. We went, of course, and the look of astonishment on his face when he caught sight of his loyal fan that far from home was a delight to behold!

I graduated from fan to friend years ago — but basically, I'm still the schoolgirl who once wrote a composition called "Gushing Girl Meets Football Hero." After meeting Irving Layton in 1963 it was a long time before I came down out of the clouds. But then how often does a fan letter to a famous poet result in a friendship that has lasted, so far, for almost thirty years!

DOROTHY RATH

Avant Midi Avec un Faune

Add living water issuing at boil
gain instant convert!
than whom there is no one more zealous
or suffers more jealousy to know
each pore and fibre,
every shade of meaning hid
in adamant thrust of unshamed black and white

Now,
in room still curtained against the night,
while the clockwork sun climbs as on an ordinary day,
I slip into facile rehypnosis
with the pristine weight upon my knee
of the gospel according to saint Irving,
seeking a clue, a thread
to bind, to hold across miles
and calendars of days and maybe ever —
sure only of the Hodgsonesque compassion,
— and unsure still without that mouth to say —
burning with need to identify
with mirroring poem —
to communicate —
knowing too late the inadequacy of a proffered name
that winds of time will sweep from memory
before it falls beneath that eye again.
I peer through difficult page windows, echo-peepholed,
at the goat's feet, pan-ic smile —
feel again my entrails jolt and squirm
at eagle's impartial glance

till brash knocking breaks the spell
and I, guiltily loin-conscious,

caught with paper lover,
take daily bread and cake at the opened door,
seeing with bemused eyes the blatant full-blown day
around and through the stolid delivery boy
— mere flesh and blood!

March 23, 1963

FRAMING LAYTON

David Solway

> Expose thyself, thou covered nest
>   Of passions, and be seen;
> Stir up thy brood, that in unrest
>   Are ever piping keen.
> Ah! what a motley multitude,
>   Magnanimous and mean.
>
> — *Charles Heavysege*

> For such a one everything that is imagined exists or can exist,
> whereas that which does not enter within the net of imagina-
> tion is in his opinion non-existent and incapable of existing.
> — *Moses Maimonides*

Let me begin anecdotally. I first heard of Irving Layton when I was fourteen, chugging on Lac de Sable (in my hometown of Ste. Agathe) in Henry Moscovitch's three horsepower chaloupe. Henry, a precocious and talented protégé of Layton's, used to spend his summer vacations in the Laurentians. At this time he was preparing his first slim volume of bourgeois-bashing poetry (*The Serpent Ink*), and would regularly putter me out to the middle of the lake, turn off the motor, and read interminably from a blackbound portfolio of terse vituperations that he called po-ems — he had Layton's crisp accents down pat. Occasionally he interspersed these pieces with resonating verse proclamations of his sexual exploits, testimony to the power of the poetic imagination and to his fidelity as Layton's amanuensis. I must admit that my complicity was motivated by other concerns, namely the hope that Henry, the scion of a wealthy bourgeois family, might from time to time relent, swing the big mega-horsepower inboard out of the boathouse, and take me water skiing. But I paid exorbitantly for these brief episodes of genuine fun by a summerful of becalmed, lacustrine recitations which constituted my first exposure to the Muse. I discovered that poets were privileged beings, feared by society, honoured by posterity, anointed by God, indefatigably potent, and overwhelmed by the adulterous ministrations of bored, lascivious, middle-class wives. It was at that point that I first began meditating a career as a poet, learning at second hand from Henry what he assured me he had absorbed from the Master himself. As further corroboration he quoted prodigiously from the sibylline texts Layton had regularly schlepped into class, the works of the Romantic triumvirate who justified the splendour and necessity of imaginative commitment, Blake, Nietzsche and Lawrence, none of whom, as a country school hooky player, I had ever heard of. But the gap in my education was amply filled by Henry's motorboat tutorials and the loan of Layton's early books. And in fact the very first poem I ever committed *voluntarily* to memory was Layton's "The Cold Green Element" which, as Henry's captive if not entirely captivated audience, sweating under the hot sun in the middle of the lake while my tormentor read endlessly from his bulging folder, wanting nothing more than to dive into the water, I would recite inwardly to myself, especially the conclusion:

> And misled by the cries of young boys
>   I am again
> A breathless swimmer in that cold green element.

Four years later, as a student living in Montreal, I attended one of Layton's night classes at Sir George Williams University. I was no longer the country neophyte inhabiting that ambiguous region between awe and boredom into which poetry had inducted me, but a practising poetaster in my own right, bristling with convictions and a sense of adolescent infallibility. Moreover, as a student of Louis Dudek, I had become aware of the hothouse conflict between Dudek and Layton which divided the aspirant community of young poets into roving partisan bands doing battle in the cloakroom of Redpath Library and in the pages of *The McGill Daily*. I was at the time a loyal Dudekin, arrogant with sceptical modesty, heaping scorn and animadversion on the company of mad Laytonians who were immediately conspicuous by the fact that they all affected Layton's clipped, oddly British pronunciation, were "Fanatic in belief some rival / Mode of metaphor lacks wit and style," chewed garlic and onions with revolutionary ardour, and slathered their conversation with the names of Blake, Nietzsche and Lawrence. I decided it was high-time to check out the firebreathing Moloch who devoured young poets for breakfast or turned them into diminutive clones of his own fulminating presence.

What I encountered was totally unexpected. There, holding forth at the head of the class, short, built like a wedge and resembling a boxer, strode a veritable pedagogic titan. A lordly, megaphonic rhetoric with the "wonderful claiming power" of Sara Jeannette Duncan's Dr. Drummond carried across the entire room, so that, sitting in the back row, I felt catapulted to the front, vulnerable, stripped of saving anonymity. But it was the *subtlety*, the fine distinctions he so adroitly manipulated within the protagonistic delivery, that extorted unwilling respect and admiration. The poem under discussion was Randall Jarrell's "The Death of The Ball-Turret Gunner," which I had read with much appreciation and little understanding. Layton proceeded to analyze the poem with such delicacy of insight, probing carefully and lovingly to its metaphoric core (which had escaped me entirely), that I had the uncanny feeling of listening in to the author's own thought processes, as if I were present at the act of composition itself. This was not criticism but telepathy, a transferring of the self into the privacy of another mind, which only the very greatest of teachers is capable of performing. And I was aware even then of the irony tacit in the performance, considering the notoriety of Layton's robust, basilican and narcissistic poetic ego. I had (and have) seldom observed so gracious and productive a deference of self to the work of another. I learned many things in that class. I learned more about the complex operations of metaphor in an hour than I had in years of reading — I continue to bring Jarrell's poem as an illustration of the metaphoric principle to the attention of my own students to this day. But perhaps most importantly, I learned that love of life and literature has many forms, and is by no means cancelled or compromised by the driving, aggressive, flamboyant manifestation of self associated with the poetic ego in need of confirmation. Not that Layton's really needed it. Jarrell has said that if a poet is struck by lightning six times, he is a genius. Layton has been *charred* by lightning innumerable times — even a dubious Elspeth Cameron gives him fifteen "world-class poems" — so that he bears a metaphorical resemblance to the tree in "The Cold Green Element" "for whom the lightning was too much / and grew a brilliant / hunchback with a crown of leaves." (However, all this notwithstanding, I did not return for the second part of the class, sensing the danger inherent in prolonged exposure to so powerful and *vortical* a personality.)

I finally got around to meeting this strange, promethean hybrid, this nemesis / benefactor, quite by accident some three or four years later halfway around the world. I had rented a villa for the summer on the island of Mallorca, in a tiny hamlet called Fornalutx tucked away in the mountains to the northeast. Now in my early twenties, I had come close to the conclusion that one could do nothing great in Canada (forgetting Layton's example), and that for an aspiring young Canadian writer expatriation was the only solution to citizenship. After six weeks or so, I reluctantly admitted to myself that not only was I doing nothing great, I was doing nothing at all, with the result that I spent most of my days sitting outside the village café drinking brandy and coffee, and at least feeling like a writer if not being one. It was during one of these dusty, mesembrian sessions that I noticed a taxi pull up across the street and disgorge three very uncomfortable passengers, one of whom I seemed to recognize: a short, bullish man addressing everyone in his immediate vicinity in a huge, oratorical voice, pounding away like a Mobilfacta compressor on an Ikea display platform, commenting on the heat, the dust, the glazed enamel of the sky, the remoteness of the village, and didn't Robert Graves live around here, a fine poet and mythographer but somewhat lacking as a novelist, and where was the house he had been promised, why was there nobody to meet him, could that be construed as neglect? "Let's ask *him*," said Bill Goodwin, Layton's nephew, pointing in my direction, and Aviva Layton inquired as to the condition of my English.

My first encounter with Layton and his party did not begin auspiciously. I could not help him immediately locate the house which had been put at his disposal, and Bill considered that they should perhaps backtrack to Soller, the nearest large town. How far is Soller from here, Bill wanted to know. About six miles as the crow flies, I replied. Well, we don't intend to fly, Bill remarked witheringly, and Layton grunted in approval. Smarting under the rebuke, feeling more and more like a Canadian and less and less like a writer, intimidated by the proximity of greatness, I left the table and scampered around the village like Carroll's unicorn, asking everyone I met about a mysterious empty house awaiting visitors. This, I realized, was a crucial moment in my development as a poet, once again, as if 'to the clanging tunes of appetite and chance,' implicated with Layton's charismatic presence, and if I were to fail in my quest — the phrase 'triumph of accommodation' ran through my head — I might as well turn in my ambitions and become rich. Fate intervened in the guise of the local blacksmith, who had been informed by the owner of the house and was able to give me precise directions. And so it was that I led the great poet in a triumph of accommodation to the door of his sanctum, receiving in return the benediction of his "good work" and a remark about the appropriateness of the blacksmith — Blake's Urthona, Joyce's forging Dedalus — as a metaphor of the poet. (Layton's comment in his poem "Fornalutx" was untypically laconic: "The house, of course, was decent enough." The town, however, he situated in one of Dante's bituminous circles.)

Later in the afternoon we gathered at the reservoir for a swim. This concrete rectangle, filled with weedy, brackish water, sat in a kind of coulee or arroyo about a kilometre out of town in the direction of Deya where Robert Graves held court. I had heard that Graves was throwing a party that evening for friends and members of the local intelligentsia, but neither Layton nor I had been invited. "One must be magnanimous," Layton observed, "he probably doesn't know I'm here." This led to a discussion of Graves and his work — "a considerable poet," Layton conceded. Across the valley from the reservoir rose the grey mass of the highest mountain in the northern chain, which Layton speculated was the source of one of Graves' most celebrated poems, "Rocky Acres," a meticulously descriptive work , a piece of mood-painting. I suggested rather timorously that the descriptive aspect of the poem was entirely pretextual, that the mountain could only be regarded as inadvertent, and that what Graves was actually providing was a detailed mindscape, a pictorial representation of the spiritual dimension in which he lived, somewhat like Hopkins' sonnet 42. I went on at some length, recalling Layton's own exegesis of Jarrell, and was gratified and relieved by his willingness to listen and his approval of my hermeneutic efforts. I have never forgotten that day in Fornalutx, partly because it was the day on which I first began to feel a preliminary sense of confirmation in that elusive adequacy of self which underlies all the madness and

ostentation of the persona. I was never a student, a disciple or a
protégé of Layton's, but I benefitted enormously from the mere
generosity of his presence — despite the evident dangers. The
inveterate talker was also the most stringent and encouraging of
listeners — if, that is, you had something to say.

Ten years elapsed before I saw Layton again, this time in another
small village on another remote island, as if our encounters had
somehow been ordained to be fleeting and insular, *intersections*,
really, rather than *meetings*. Layton was spending the summer of 1973
in Molivos (not an island, as Elspeth Cameron assumes, but a village)
on the island of Lesbos where I had also rented a house, about five
kilometres outside the town in a gaggle of dwellings dignified by the
name of Eftalou (Seven Hills). To add to the strangeness of the time,
Bill and Aviva were also there, so that summer we spent in one
another's company had a weird, orchestrated air, like something
scripted, revised and polished by an unknown hand. I can't explain
how these peculiar things happen except to suggest that certain
places tend obscurely to attract certain writers at certain moments
in their careers by a kind of co-ordinate magnetism. In the short time
I spent on Lesbos (actually, in Eftalou), I met the Greek novelist
Nasos Theophilos, was introduced to the Danish poet Henrik
Nordtbrand, entertained Andy Wainwright on my front porch,
drank with Henry Sarr and crossed paths if not swords with Peter
Green. In the serendipitous light of these occasions, the fact that
Layton and I should have found ourselves once more within hailing
distance in faraway places should have been entirely predictable.

I do not have the space or leisure here to provide even a digest of
a summer's worth of discussion, argument and speculation, except
to say that with Layton life is never dull. Admittedly, I would
sometimes try to avoid meeting him on my shopping expeditions
into town if only to preserve a sense of beleaguered equanimity, for
Layton was always either on the verge of knocking off another
masterpiece or had already completed several between breakfast and
late-morning coffee. "David, my boy," he would call from his café
table, when I had not succeeded in dodging into the nearest lane or
arcade, "I've caught two fish already, one big, one small," leaving me
to ponder the fate of the minnow I had struggled with all morning,
thrumps of groupers shoaling by the mind's eye. Sometimes I might
be invited for a cup of coffee, and if I demurred, I was immediately

assured the coffee was *at his expense*: there could be, in other words, no compelling reason for refusal. (Much later, when reading *Waiting for the Messiah*, I couldn't help but smile over the passage in which Layton writes that he felt "privileged to pay for" Jack Stern's coffee.) Nor could I explain that my reluctance derived from the need to protect what Coleridge called the 'initiative,' the first slender hint and impulse of a poetic phrase or rhythm, from Layton's philharmonic obliterations. How many poems have I lost to Layton's generous invitations I cannot afford to calculate.

But even though the 'relationship' had changed over the years and I no longer felt myself to be the eternally grateful catechumen, I was still to some extent an apprentice and could profit immeasurably from his example. The form of insecurity that troubled me at this time had nothing to do with the vocational doubt of the earlier years and everything to do with whether I was practising my craft in the right contemporary way. I was not only partial to rhyme and enamoured of stanzaic intricacies, but I also counted syllables on an internal abacus and would sometimes tell beats and accents on a set of worry-beads I kept for the purpose. Could anything be more misguided and preposterous? The poets of my generation spoke of open-ended lines, semantically charged energy fields, and projective verse à la Olson, of the curse of the definite article à la Rostrover Hamilton, of the fragmentation of the modern sensibility reflected in paratactic utterance à la Fenellosa, and of subtle laparophonic euphonies and wispy internal rhymes à la just about everybody, whereas I seemed to be concerned mainly with the staid, orthodox three Rs of the discipline: Reading, Riting and Rhythmitic. I brazened on impenitently but much of my apparent conviction and indifference was merely protective camouflage.

One afternoon Layton, Bill and Aviva arrived in Eftalou for a visit which, as the day careened on in typical Greek fashion, turned into a multi-course meal punctuated by frequent trips to the retsina barrel. After a couple of hours I noticed that Layton was absent — or rather, I noticed that I no longer noticed him, an unlikely event in itself. Somewhat apprehensive, I set off in search, recalling an acquaintance who had fallen from the cliffs further up the road and spent six weeks recuperating in the Mytilini hospital. I need not have worried. There was Layton sitting cross-legged on the beach, a notepad open beside him, and a pencil in one hand; the other hand served as a time-keeper, fingers toting up the syllables. Then the tip of his pencil began tapping faintly against a pebble, like a fairy tuning fork lightly striking the rim of a martini glass. Layton was counting his syllables, he was measuring out iambs and anapests, he was calling his words to order, he was tallying stress and accent like clusters of his own red chokecherries for the sake of 'perfection of form.' Here was the Layton whom many, naïve readers or detractors — having in a failure of accommodation bought the *enfant terrible* persona wholesale — refused to acknowledge or acclaim: the strict, responsible *maker* or *poiitis* who crafted the nifty Hudibrastics of "Prologue to The Long Pea Shooter," or the deft, ergonomic stanzas of sonnets like "When It Came To Santayana's Turn," "Icarus," "A Strange Turn," and "The Antipodeans," or the honey-tight perfection of "Early Morning in Mithymna," the poet (as Brian Trehearne in the fine Introduction to Layton's most recent volume, *Fornalutx*, correctly remarks) whose "striking casualness of tone . . . disguises the meticulousness of rhythmic expression . . ." And as I watched from the shade of a plane tree, I was again confirmed in my congenial practice. From that point on in our relationship, the intimidating Layton became the avuncular Irving, one of the selves in the repertoire I have been most privileged to know.

Hinge

It is almost twenty years since that summer in Lesbos and Irving Layton, with his plumbline and basket of fruit, is now my neighbour. Predictably, this means we practically never see each other except for an occasional beer or fitness swimming at the YMCA pool, a distant relative of the Fornalutx reservoir. I find after all this time that I know a fair amount about the work but almost nothing about the man, despite the proliferation of biographical material. What *do* I know? I surmise that Irving Layton is now eighty, since I have attended his seventy-fifth birthday celebration for five consecutive years. I know that he is as passionate, vigorous, eloquent, engaging, and rancorous in his dislikes as ever. I recognize that the creative artist in him, both wise and splenetic, shares something with the playful and destructive temperament of the child, refusing the desiccations of a merely prudential maturity — tending, as Carlos Fuentes enjoins, "the savage ocean he bears within because it's the only thing left to him

of two overlapping creations: that of the world and that of the child."
(The desideratum, Fuentes says, is "not to dry out.") I know that he
is immortal. But I'm not sure where to locate the source of that
Lupercalian vitality which swells and quickens his poetry and is
responsible for a staunchless productivity that sometimes leads to
dilution, crambo and repetitiveness, but which makes the best of the
poems almost self-memorizing. What is it about the *quality* of the
essential work which renders it unique in the history of our literature? Other Canadian poets have written exceptional lines and
remarkable poems, at a lower incidence of frequency perhaps; even
so, some crucial attribute is too often missing in the latter. Is the
property of paradoxical candour one finds in lines like "and when I
write my lying poems know I am using / an anodyne from which the
fastidious man recoils"? Is it the sheer *magnitude* of the oeuvre, of
the work and the presence — which differentiates it from that of our
"North American Poet[s]" easing "self-contempt by writing verse"
— miming the burly confidence of an old-time luxobarge in a
swarming traffic of econocars? Is it the pathos, the compassion, of "I
want to climb the highest rooftop / in the village / and announce to
all / that no one in it will ever die."? The quotable lines remain
inexhaustible, so that in writing about Layton one is always in danger
of behaving like an anthology.

I suspect that the quality I am looking for has something to do
with what Jacques Derrida, borrowing a term from plainsong, calls
the *neume*, that species of vocalization that whiffles "between cry and
speech, animal and man," a language which, in Derrida's phrase, is
"uncontaminated by supplementarity," retaining in its momentum
and inevitability a trace of some original plenitude that constantly
recedes, eluding the critic and the imitator. It is a language that takes
its origin not in contract or agreement, in the prose of our quotidian
transactions (as does the bulk of contemporary poetry) but in the
irruption of the sense of *festival*, the "pure presence" of joy , rage and
celebration, the plunge into the conjugal amalgam of the Creation.
Thus it is, paradoxically, not a fully finished language in the sense of
a medium hospitable to logical discriminations, a mere disruptive
accuracy, but a language that is constantly *being born*, a pure
vocalization which, as Derrida claims, "is inspired in us by God and
may address only Him," uncorrupted by interval and discontinuity.
This may account for the feeling one often has in the presence of

great poetry, as in the best of Layton's work, that one is not listening or reading directly: *one is eavesdropping.* And this is why, too, before the talismanic power of the word, there is, finally, little to be said that is neither performative nor anecdotal: emulation, repeating out loud what one has heard, indulging in the higher gossip.

The voice of the neume, diffracted into the myriad articulations of grim lament and pure doxology, is the language of restoration, of the discovery and recovery of all that suffers the attrition of an increasingly worried, mundane and banausic age. As a young poet, at least marginally influenced by Layton's vision and practice, I once dedicated to him a humble quatrain with the disproportionate title, "Coda to the Twentieth Century":

The minotaur gorges on human pork;
the blood of Theseus sweetens the dish.
Impaled on Poseidon's practical fork
Odysseus goes to feed the fish.

Layton's central awareness is that we are living in a thin, demythologized time that lacks, for all its technological aplomb and its conquest of the natural world, a sense of mythic grandeur, sustaining heroism and epical vitality. ("Runts are the problem, / runts who long for the stride and stature / of giants . . .") It is precisely these deficits that Layton's Muse has determined to remedy and supply. Blake, Nietzsche and Lawrence are his immediate progenitors but the lineage he honours and redeems goes back to Theseus who confronts the teratologies of human corruption, and to Odysseus who resists the envious and reductive temper of the age in which he navigates. Somewhere between Poseidon and the minotaur, the afflicting and representative god on the one hand and, on the other, the brutal deformities of the contemporary self, the neumic language of genuine poetry sings and curses in its festival of revival. This is Layton's gift and calling, the source of his authority as a poet, accounting for the tone of carnival exuberance which animates his work as it alienates a progressively empirical audience. And if one objects to the Theseus-and-Odysseus citation as archaic and inappropriate, perhaps one can take Layton at his own word as a mischievous and resuscitated 'Dionysus in Hampstead' who looks about him at the diminished spectacle of modernity and observes:

The wise and the just are too solemn
under their long shadows they do not dance
at the weddings I hear in the grass
at the mock funerals I hear in the leaves of trees.

Or as the proleptic mystic of many other poems, the one who asks
where

are gone the grizzled ecstatic
  faces
    of the vehement crazy men
who dreamed and prayed?

And if the reader should dismiss my reference to Derrida's concept
of the neume to characterize Layton's "wild peculiar joy" as improbable, I would direct him or her to Roland Barthes' complementary
notion of the "grain of the voice," that elusive yet unmistakable
"something which is . . . in the cavities, the muscles, the membranes,
the cartilages . . . The grain is . . . the materiality of the body
speaking its mother tongue." Although Barthes alludes to the actual
voice raised in song and not to the written word *per se*, his distinctions strike me as eminently applicable to the rich carnality of the
poetic line, heard in the mind's ear as one reads, or compelling one
to reproduce the texture of the composing voice itself, to revel in "the
voluptuousness of its sound-signifiers" as in the syllables of a beloved
name (which, in Layton's words, "ignite each other / . . . to let music
and flame / astonish the whole world.") The "grain" is that which
denies reductive codification and holds in check precisely what
"average culture" wants: prosaic, acceptable and merely decent
articulation. What Layton gives us, on the contrary, is the neumic
recrudescence of creative ardour in a language that hovers between
cry and speech, or alternatively, in Barthes' formulation, the quality
of the grain which is "the body in the voice as it sings, the hand as it
writes, the limb as it performs." Perhaps it all comes down in the end
to the archetypal yet increasingly rare sense of creative gratitude we
find in Bede's Caedmon who sings Creation, praising the "Work of
the world-warden, wonder of wonders." Or in Layton's "Elephant,"
who has learned "the necessary art / of converting irritation into
pleasure" and whose "ecstasy rotundity / and gratuitous weight /
make proportionate to his itch," generating his "rapturous blare.'"

Panel 2

In the first part of this essay I spoke of my episodic meetings or intersections with Layton in order to counter one of the most persistent cliches that circulate around his name. Many people find Layton, both in his verse and *in propria persona*, too loud, pushy, orgulous and self-referential for comfort (as if he embodied his own description of Norman Bethune in *Waiting for the Messiah*: "Here was a man who seemed to be devoured by an idea, an obsession. He did not seem a man with whom one could be comfortable. Some people found him attractive, others, for the same reasons, were repelled.") They object to what they read as an unmediated exhibition of the self, a preputial rhetoric lacking measure or discretion, a display of biblical postures and invectives that are either needlessly abrasive or embarrassingly inappropriate. Detractors will often recall Eliot's strictures against the intervention of the biographical self (Layton, of course, cannot abide Eliot, "at best, a single hair / from the beard of Dostoevsky") or Wallace Stephens writing in "Adagia," *Opus Posthumous*, "The poet confers his identity on the reader. But he cannot do this if he intrudes personally." Layton, after all, just about out-Mailers Mailer in his advertisements for himself, and those fortunate enough to have received the occasional letter from the master may recall Layton's face stencilled on the envelope, somewhat larger than the Queen's stamped beside it. I, too, must confess to random moments of disbelief at the spectacle of what might appear as an unmitigated hybris; times when I grew convinced I was confronting a certifiable Romaniac. And sometimes I was hard put to detect evidence of that "exigent and censorious taste" (in Lionel Trilling's lapidary phrase) in the man who claimed to have discovered sex for his fellow Canadians and flaunted his luck "to be loved / by the one girl / in this Presbyterian country / who knows how to give / a man pleasure" (hyperbole notwithstanding); who in an act of unprecedented humility conceded "No, I'll never / be greater than William Shakespeare"; whose famous profession of poetic modesty with regard to nature's divided things — "I am their mouth; as a mouth I serve" — sounds a little less apostolic than derivative (poetry, said Rilke, is "a mouth which else Nature would lack"); and whose striving for effect will often betray a surprising inability to gauge or adjust means to ends, leading to the bathos of over-kill:

> I want you to feel as if I had slammed
>   your child's head against a spike;
> And cut off your member and stuck it in your
>   wife's mouth to smoke like a cigar . . .

(George Woodcock reacts with "puzzled wonder that so good a poet could write . . . such wretched verse," and invokes the Peter-and-Petrushka principle, the poet as Saturnalian clown-king, to explain the conundrum.) All this is true, I'm afraid, but also false — in the sense that it leaves out *at least* as much as it purports to cover. For a proper, balanced appreciation of Irving Layton requires that the serious reader *frame the name* with quotation marks, despite what friends, critics, title pages and telephone directories may claim. *There is, in fact, no such person as Irving Layton.* The self has fused into the persona whose full, authoritative and final name is "Irving Layton," the last in a series of pseudonyms, the name of a neo-Whitmanian fiction who is large, who contains multitudes, and who may contradict himself with epistemic impunity. This is why it is inadvisable to condemn "Layton" for surface infelicities, lapses of taste or sudden changes of thematic direction: one risks making a fool of oneself. The writer who doubts that he will ever transcend Shakespeare remains fully aware of the absurdity of the concession, incorporating both the manifest bombast and the underlying subtlety as elements constituting the persona. ("Damn that unscalable pinnacle / of excellence mocking our inevitable / inferiority and failure . . ." As if the only effective way of escaping obliteration is via humour. Or, perhaps, apotheosis, Matthew Arnold's strategy, for whom Shakespeare makes the "Heaven of Heavens his dwelling-place." "Layton's" title directs us back to Arnold's tame capitulation on which the later poem must be read in part as a playful and rambunctious commentary.) The poet who is notorious for the tympany of self-election is the same poet who writes the compassionate and immortal "For Keine Lazarovitch" or the unforgettable "O Jerusalem" which concludes with the central question of our duplicitous humanity:

> And how may we walk upon this earth
>   with forceful human stir
> unless we betray you and adore?

How can the same poet write with the inevitable precision of feeling and form, the verbal etiquette we find in "An Old Niçoise Whore" and then produce a few poems later in the same volume the thumb-in-the-soup piece called "Westminster Abbey" unless it is attempted *in some sense* deliberately or with informed awareness, the mask embracing the whole of our paragon-of-animals to quintes-sence-of-dust humanity, all the glory, jest and riddle of it — by choice? The poet is shrewdly conscious of what he is about, as he himself confesses in a letter to Milton Wilson of 9th June, 1963, in which he affirms the necessity of donning an outrageous mask in so featureless a culture as ours.

The entire panoramic sweep of Blakean contraries extends before us in the work of this extraordinary poet, from the "five neat graves in a semicircle" spawned by Père Loisel in "Côte Des Neiges Cemetery" to the "five glorious cherubs / [a]float in the waves" in "The Sweet Light Strikes My Eyes," from the linnet *under* rock in "Still Life" to the butterfly *on* rock in the poem of that name — each visionary bracket making up that "exciting composition" of contrar-ies, complementary oppositions, frailties and strengths, smallnesses and catholicities, that he himself observes in "Sheep":

> And I myself at my wife's deathbed
> Shall, I know, weep: weep like Othello, be
>   grief-rent and troubled

Yet note the small cost of some extra flowers or bulbs.
And how can we be sure that the composite, ostensible self which intrudes so robustly and with such pectoral swagger into one poem after another, like a weightlifter in a locker room, is neither more nor less that an intentional *effect*, a contrived and intricate prosthetic device, an expression not of the muscular bully of the personal self *but of a personally-intrusive, self-aggrandizing persona*, merely one more feature of the protagonistic fiction which can no longer be distinguished from the reality? AND which, even in its most steroidal forms, carries the same 'value' or validity as the subtle, wise and empathic recorder of the human pageant, the transcendent scribe mentioned by Ezekiel who, clothed with linen and with a writer's inkhorn at his side, accompanies the group of men with slaughter weapons in their hands. (It is, after all, the scribe who is commanded

to go in between the wheels of the cherubim and fill his hands with coals of fire. As "Layton" writes in "Esthétique," "poems that love the truth tell / All things have value being combustible.") Thus, in responding as readers to the composite and contradictory, specular illusion of "Irving Layton" (the bearer of a Negative Capability which, as Keats attested, may include even the "unpoetical") with sufficient passion and engagement, whether gratitude, approval, respect, dislike, revulsion, or even a sort of styptic ambivalence, we hypostatize the fiction, confer reality upon the name which now represents a collective hallucination from which neither reader nor writer may disengage himself. It is almost as if, in repudiation of Lampman's facile conclusion to "The Clearer Self," "Layton" understood that the isomorphic phrases, "the clearer self, the grander me," simply don't work for him as conceptual appositions, and are in fact more likely to be mutually inhospitable than reinforcing. Rather, the sources of that immense vitality, of "the grander me," lies in a kind of pluralistic élan, like his own "Artist-God who shapes and plays with . . . infinite variety" and with the "joyous impermanency" of the innumerable forms of existence, incorporated into the poetic ego.

For "Layton" has been possessed, in a Bloomian sense, by a pleroma of archontic selves: the loving father ("Poem for My Daughter"), the bitter satirist ("From Colony to Nation"), the tender and compassionate lover ("Berry Picking"), the erotic imperialist ("Nausicaa"), the quintessential poet ("The Birth of Tragedy"). A throng of lesser or commonplace selves is also present, part of the unedited 'humanity' to which the work bears theatrical and often strident witness. With "Layton," it's the whole bloody bird, or bard. Chauvinist, bully, mythographer, elegist, worshipper, tyrant and servant, ultimately he transcends possession and becomes, *veritably becomes*, that daemonic succession of voices, characters, phases, phrases and multiple nictitating selves (like an updated version of Rameau's Nephew) collected in his nearly fifty volumes, so that the category of the 'real' blends and coalesces with that of the imagination, the 'imaginary-imaginative.' One could quite plausibly interpret "Layton" as the objectification of the Lacanian ego which — as Lacan writes — "is absolutely impossible to distinguish from the imaginary captures which constitute it . . ."

Abrogating the distinction between text and life, "Layton" must finally be approached as a poetic event or phenomenon, a powerful and consistently inconsistent self-improvisation whose impact on others (whether as readers or interlocutors) is never merely benign and necessarily entails consequences. Thus it is futile and irrelevant to object to "Layton," as so many have done, on pragmatic or narrowly ethical grounds, for one must understand him as the *Compleat Man* (or Mangler) in the most radical sense of the term, a thesaurus of synonymous contraries self-defined in various poems as a "cringing semite" with a "hot Hebrew heart," as a "quiet madman never far from tears" smugly and with vicarious bluster paging Mr. Superman. This is not a "life" with a psychological centre in the ordinary sense; this is rhetoric incarnate, a *dramatis personae* of both effective and embarrassing roles and masks, "today Bluebeard, tomorrow / Babbitt," to quote James Merrill, an abstraction blooded by belief in immaculate beginnings, a "cold-eyed artist" who in his own words "finds enjoyment in contemplating the infinite theatrical shapes life so lavishly creates" and who attains in the fullness of his career to the status of the Demonical Sublime.

For it is precisely the fourth of Harold Bloom's revisionary ratios which comes closest to explaining the phenomenon of "Irving Layton." I refer once again to the category of Demonization, which Bloom defines as "a mythification of the father . . . purchased by withdrawal from the self, at the high price of dehumanization." "Layton" has incorporated and rewritten the seminal or initiating texts which go by the name of Blake, Nietzsche and Lawrence, setting up as Counter-Sublime a self-constructed, legendary presence: the sonorous, oratorical voice, the clear, unCanadian elocution, the studied magnanimity of gaze and gesture clouded suddenly with prophetic fury and denunciation, the grandeur of phrase doubly conspicuous in common circumstance, the familiar citations from the illustrious dead, the calorific greeting and valedictory rodomontade, and the sense of apodictic assurance, of absolute lexical confidence, all of which go to make up his aura. And of such poets who share the antithetical burden of greatness, a Shelley, a Blake, a Yeats, a Layton, (to use the names straight) one can merely say that the most 'human' quality they possess, perhaps the only 'human' thing about them, is their death — the one power which escapes recruitment and is therefore a match for the daemonization of the ego, which in turn is rendered all the more human for its poignant fragility.

As for the question of the managerial self, the gerundive essence, which molds and manipulates the mask and is responsible for the *trompe l'oeil* of an impersonating presence, this is something that cannot be addressed, for the epistemological recession is endless, red-shifted out of reach. "[B]efore all my arrogant poems," writes Whitman, "the real Me stands yet untouch'd . . .," a remark whose meaning resides not only in explicit content but also in the piety of nostalgia or regret. The fact remains, as with most of the poets we honour with the sobriquet 'great,' we have to frame the name with inverted commas as we do the titles of the poems that cluster round that name, since in the last analysis they behave like identical, interchangeable fictions, orbiting one another like satellites around an invisible centre. As for the "real Me," it either does not exist, or exists but cannot be addressed, which amounts to the same thing.

It thus becomes almost beside the point to quibble over an objectionable "Layton," to restrict him from our personal libraries or our imaginations, while extending the favour of our conventional regard to the laundered, acceptable, innocuous 'great' whom an F.R. Leavis might have duly vetted into the tradition. With "Layton," the word and the event in all their multiplicity have coincided and merged to become one and the same thing, which is, when you come to think of it, the meaning of the Hebrew term *davar*, a term whose appositeness in context is self-evident. Word and event, work and life struggle to encompass the entire body of the world while there is still time, to produce the "saint, madman, fool" of one poem, the "seer, sensualist, or fake ambassador" of another, wishing to become "all one, / existence seamless . . ." In the last analysis "Layton" is not so much a person as a force, a kind of verbal hurricane whose "rapturous eye" evades detection but in whose radial sweep can be found all the treasure and debris which make up his Collected Works, the poems as well as the selves — the "daimons," he tells us in *The Gucci Bag*, that he is "impatient to greet."

Troubling as his manifold, declamatory presence may sometimes appear to us, whether as legislator or seeker, as gadfly to the critics, self-appointed conscience to Canadians, or Covering Cherub to his younger competitors, I think our final response should be one of gratitude for the fact that he is among us. For what other Canadian poet has given us such sensual and ironic poems as these, poems to

David Solway and Irving Layton at reunion and launching of *CIV/n:*
A Literary Magazine of the 50s, 5 March 1983.

discomfit "the pragmatic vegetables in their stands" — poems, that is, which pack a *political* wallop, attacking both our consensual anonymity and the arrogance of ignorance, poems that have probed to the Schikelgruber depths of all of us, victor and victim alike? That have so candidly and unsparingly confessed "the anodyne from which fastidious men recoil" and at the same time blessed the "sweet light" in poetical hosannas for the transfigurations of joy it confers upon us. Poems dying down into love without "disquiet or passion" only to be re-ignited by "genital electricity," testifying to the antinomies that both disrupt and glorify even the meanest of lives. It is probably clear to us by this time that without "Layton" to revile and esteem, to condemn and praise, to dismiss as a raving narcissist or exalt as one of our Promethean benefactors, without that *summa* of many conflicting selves, gentle and abrasive, blessed and damned, this country would be all the poorer, all the more devitalized,

> like an unoccupied chair in the park
> like brown grass without water
> or trees without birds . . .

IRVING LAYTON:
A TRIBUTE

Shula Steinberg

I had lived in Canada for about a year and a half, in Calgary and Winnipeg, when my parents decided to move once again, this time to Montreal. So in 1955, with the financial help of the Canadian Jewish Congress (my parents were keen on my Jewish education), I enrolled in grade seven at Herzliah, a Jewish parochial school in Montreal. Irving Layton turned out to be my classroom teacher. My first recollection of Layton was his great warmth and smile. He made me feel so welcome, quite a contrast from my classmates. But then, how can I really blame them? My parents and I were newly arrived immigrants from Israel and survivors of the Holocaust, and these were upper middle class kids. I recall one compassionate classmate taking me to her home and giving me some of her own clothes.

What I remember most about Irving Layton was his obsession with reading poetry. I was not aware as yet that he was a poet and so found it somewhat strange for a teacher to often begin a class (whether it be English, Latin, or Algebra, by reading poems to the class). Layton also bombarded the class with political and religious questions. I remember one day he actually took a count as to how many of us believed in God and how many did not. Most of the class voted in the affirmative. I abstained. When he asked me why I had chosen to abstain, my answer was that I had not as yet made up my mind. Layton jumped for joy, his eyes lighting up with excitement, saying that mine was the most intelligent answer.

Layton's manner of teaching, I believe, was in keeping with the Hebrew prophets. His passion for social justice was something that to this day keeps ringing in my ears, and his anger about man's inhumanity to man was solidly engraved in my consciousness. He showed great disdain for any kind of propaganda and media influence. I especially recall his outrage at the way the media treated the Russians. I have vivid memories of his description of Russian people as warm and loving and having the same needs as the Americans.

Having lived in Russia for four years myself, it was easy for me to relate to what he was saying. But the Cold War was in full force at that time and his statements, I believe, were taken out of context. Eventually, because of this, the students' parents labelled him a communist and made life quite difficult for him. This, however, took place after I had left the school.

From time to time Layton would walk into the classroom with poetry books, most of them his own. I remember him selling his own poetry books for about fifty or seventy-five cents a piece, but when it came time for me to buy one (which I always offered to) he would put one of his poetry books on my desk saying it was my birthday present. I remember having quite a few birthday presents in the course of the two years that I studied with him.

When it came time to write compositions, I always struggled with words. He was very reassuring though. Irving Layton graded me differently from anyone else. He used to say that he would give me two kinds of grades. The first was for my imagination and the second for my composition. For my imagination he always gave me an "A" and for my composition anywhere from a "D" to a "C." He then averaged out my grades and the end result was that I would usually end up with a "C" or a "B."

One of the most precious memories I have were my weekly visits with him to the second floor library at Herzliah. At a time when the class busied itself with homework, Mr. Layton would take me up to the library and spend about ten to fifteen minutes introducing me to various books. I felt very special, and in time I believe, because of Mr. Layton's unique attention to me, my classmates grew to like me too. One of the very first books Layton introduced me to was Homer's *Iliad*, followed by Shakespeare's *A Midsummer Night's Dream*, and a collection of poems by Byron, Shelley, Wordsworth and his own, of course. It was part of my homework, to read as much from the selected books as I could, come back the week after and tell Mr. Layton which ones I liked and why. His purpose he said was to inspire me to love the English language, more specifically, poetry. Upon reflection, however, I feel that he also wanted me to break my silence which was always there.

In December of 1987, after many years of thinking about it, I finally had the courage to write Irving Layton a letter and thank him for being such an important person during my early years in Canada.

To my great amazement I received a reply. What struck me most was that he remembered my silence and he hoped that the years had been kinder to me.

When the weather was nice, Layton would often join us in a baseball game during recess. I would stand on the side and watch, not being familiar with the game. But this did not last long; Layton would yell in my direction and motion me to join. I grew to like baseball quite a lot after that.

Perhaps Layton's single, most important influence on me (besides the love for poetry and justice) was his love and appreciation of the visual arts. At that time he was married to Betty Sutherland and one of the things he used to share with us in class was how much he admired Betty's paintings. Ever since I can remember, I always drew, but my parents looked down upon my drawings as a fancy pastime and discouraged me from taking it seriously. Because of my great admiration and respect for Layton I, in time, began to believe that there was merit in being an artist and eventually became one myself.

In May of 1990 I received an invitation from Mr. Layton to attend his poetry reading at Harbourfront. I was very nervous to go. I had fears of losing my childhood fantasy about him. After all, this was thirty-five years later. At first Layton did not recognize me and seemed somewhat distant. So I went over and spoke with his wife Anna. I took an instant liking to her and she in turn understood my need to speak with her husband. During the reception, Anna cornered Layton to come and sit beside me. Over a drink, Layton began to remember as I recapitulated my memories of him. I told him about his gift of books, the visits to the library and how he graded my compositions. I loved watching his face light up as I told him these stories. Sitting that night beside him, surrounded by so many people and Layton giving me undivided attention, I felt once again so very special, like that young school girl back at Herzliah. I must confess that Layton then, as Layton now, has never disappointed me.

IRVING LAYTON:
A SHORT MEMOIR

Fruma Rothberg Sanders

When I crossed paths with Irving Layton, I said, "Are you Irving Layton?"

"If a young woman stops you with her smile and asks, 'Are you Irving Layton?' you answer 'Yes'," was the reply. "And who are you?"

I briefly introduced myself; I was just out of university with a Bachelor of Fine Arts degree and I was walking back to the Laura Secord store to repay the twenty cents that a storekeeper had trusted me with earlier that day. Irving wanted to come with me, to see this happening, as he thought it was incredible.

"What determines one's success as an artist?" I asked.

"One's spirit is one's destiny," answered Irving Layton.

I felt like I was reading *The Prophet* by Khalil Gibran, only it was not a passive absorption. I was at the feet of the master and we were walking down de Maisonneuve Boulevard in Montreal together. A young man came towards us.

"Hello, Irving," he said.

Smiles and pleasantries were exchanged. They chatted briefly, like old friends, and I was introduced. When they parted, Irving said, "That man was a film producer, but he has been too refined, so he has just not made it. Now he works for his mother, in her gallery. To succeed as an artist, you must be an animal, a savage," he said.

"But can't one be refined and still succeed?" I asked.

"Prove to me that I'm wrong," Irving answered.

Some artists whom Irving and I knew in common were recalled, and Irving emphasized how impressed he was with their animal spirits, which was so contrary to the orthodoxy of my background.

"Come, let us have a beer together. Your grandchildren will be more impressed if you drank beer with me, rather than tea or coffee."

I agreed, never having been in a pub. Irving pointed to a place opposite the Laura Secord shop, and, after he had been the witness to my returning twenty cents to the store, we went into the pub. We sat opposite each other, in the semi-darkness, with the red interior and the dark brown wood.

I was acutely aware of being in the company of a famous poet and surprised that there was not a signed photograph of him near the entrance. At least there should have been accolades and trumpets with Rubens-like figures to announce Irving as he took his seat. Instead, we were unobserved, anonymous.

We sipped our beers, and Irving talked about love.

"First, you create love. And then, once you have it, you destroy it," Irving mused.

I just listened, with my own experience not yet understood. I was so close to my father, who never wanted a feather to touch me, if it were to bring me harm. I was not to understand this either, until I was a parent myself. I offered to write Irving a short story, about him, our meeting; he offered a lyric poem about me.

"But the truth is that you are not Irving Layton at all," I said.

"Why . . . How did you know?" he played along with me. "I am a businessman and I just could not resist telling you that I am Irving Layton, because the opportunity came my way."

"But you seem like a poet — your hair, your leather jacket . . ."

"Businessmen of today are not what they used to be. You're thinking within a stereotype," he exuded with pride, as he pounced on my naïveté.

I was dumbfounded. We left the pub together, Irving laughing, and I puzzled by how my own game had turned about. Irving left me on the sidewalk, he taking a taxi and I pondering who this man had been, on this Friday afternoon in the summertime.

Several months later, a poetry reading by Irving Layton was advertised. I attended. When Irving Layton saw me coming into the audience, he greeted me and laughed.

"So, I really am Irving Layton after all, and I will never be able to fool you again," he joked.

We have exchanged pleasantries through the years, and I have always admired Irving's genuine support of writers, his approachability. One day, I took a bus up to the West Island and I thought of what a contrast this neighbourhood must have been to Irving, when he attended agriculture school in Ste. Anne de Bellevue, on a scholarship as a young man. When his son had been a guest at my parents' cottage in the Laurentians, our obscure ethnocentricities had been envied.

Irving did nothing quietly. His refinement as a man showed itself with the confidence of his later years. Women's complaints with feminist issues made Irving colourful, rather than a man to be spitefully rebuked. His women had not been destroyed or made to feel that they could not exist without him.

The blast that Irving made against what was then conventional thought, in the early sixties, when I was too young to understand what the issues were, made everyone angry at my blended family's Friday night dinners.

Irving, with his outspokenness, has been a threat to every establishment he has ever been aware of, and everyone has had to take notice. The voice of Amy Lowell's patterns being broken, was relevant to Victorian genres, which existed too long in Canada. Irving was obtuse, in the Canada that was too passive to agree to disagree.

And, as for my early disagreements with Irving, that refinement is not to eradicate an artist's soul; I am still looking up to Irving, and his impact has been known.

LAYTON FOR FINANCE MINISTER

Moses Znaimer

The first time I laid eyes on Irving Layton he came bounding into my classroom, athletic energy and rugged good looks, shrivelled all of us with a withering stare and before saying a word, slowly, deliberately, turned his back and stood dead still.

It was Day One of the new school year and we were fresh out of grade school, in a new building, the one and only Grade 7 class at Herzliah Junior High on the edge of Fletchers Field in Montreal, part of the UTT Parochial School system which taught the regular Protestant school board curriculum of Spelling and Math and History and English Literature, and French, in half a day, and a mix of Jewish religion, History and Literature and Hebrew grammar in the other half.

The class consisted of a majority of young girls, most from middle class, ultra-orthodox homes, clothed in tunics and woollen stockings or dresses with high collars and long sleeves down to the wrists, being prepared, you could say fattened, for marriage; some bourgeois boys from Outremont or the nouveau riche suburbs of Snowdon and Côte St-Luc; plus two tough guys from the immigrant side of town — Sydney and me — from in and around St. Urbain Street.

Finally, in the hushed silence, Mr. Layton picked up a piece of chalk and began to scratch onto the blackboard. 99.999999 . . . he filled the front board with huge figures, top to bottom, and when he'd run out of room continued on the board that ran down the right hand wall of the room . . . 999999%, he said, and then he whipped around, fixed each of us in the eye, student by student, face by face, and repeated, "99.99999999999999999% of people are Philistines!!!"

In that one instant, exactly three minutes into my first year of higher education, not really knowing exactly what that word 'Philistine' meant, but sensing somehow that it meant something average and anonymous and dreadful, I made myself a promise and said in my own head: "Not me."

Subsequently, I looked up the word and learned that Oxford's definition of a Philistine is mild enough: *someone whose "interests are material and commonplace."* But then it adds: *"the enemy into whose hands one may fall."* That is close to what Irving conveyed to me in that one blinding, formative instant — a real anxiety, lest I fall to the bogeyman of bland and miss what he clearly regarded as the sweetness in the juicy, messy, creative turmoil of real life.

There was no mystery either, as to why Irving Layton's message to me was so instantaneously effective and subsequently memorable. He was prepared, not only to write poetry, but to be a poet, a prophet, a provocateur, a non-philistine: and to *SHOW* us that person, who he assured us was very rare; an assertion we were not disposed to challenge.

The second time I saw Irving Layton he ran into class a bit late, said he was just back from Toronto where he had launched a book and been lionized even by the CBC, and advised us to buy some of his leftover copies if we were smart. We could have them for bargain rates direct from him, the author, with no middleman. And if we didn't have the cash with us, he would grant credit provided that the twenty-five cents per book were brought in the next day and we could tell our Moms and Dads that someday his books would be collectors' items and worth a great deal of money.

Since by that time I'd heard that he was a modern poet and wrote a lot of short snappy stuff with many forbidden words, I thought, "What the Hell." And so, that day, *Music on a Kazoo*, or as we affectionately came to call it, "Music on a Cat's Ass," came into my possession for a quarter on the deferred payment plan.

In the four years subsequent, until I graduated Herzliah, I bought other stuff from Mr. Layton: *In the Midst of My Fever*, *The Bull Calf*, *The Long Pea Shooter*, *The Cold Green Element*, also know around class as "The Hot Brown Lump," *Improved Binoculars*, *The Blue Propeller*, and so on! He pushed not only his own stuff but books and little magazines full of Dudek and Souster and Acorn and Purdy and a little later, a new guy called Cohen.

Nothing ever cost more than fifty cents, and some of the Samizdat stuff went for as little as fifteen cents and in total I estimate that Mr. Layton, ruthlessly exploiting his position of glamour and power, dazzled and otherwise browbeat me, his captive student, into shell-

Batter up! Herzliah Junior High School, Montreal, spring 1952.
Photo: H.S. Adler. Irving Layton Collection, Concordia University.

ing out about four or five bucks for early contemporary, post-war Canlit; before it was called Canlit.

Now, I want to address and once and for all lay to rest this canard that poets in Canada are doomed to be eternally poor, mendicants dependent on handouts; you know, the cherished image of 'artiste' as practical idiot. Tell me about it!

A couple of weeks ago I'm reading this story in *Books in Canada* and it says "something strange is happening in the unpredictable world of rare books. First or early editions of work by some English Canadian writers are suddenly hot commodities." So I call Stephen Temple, a dealer — maybe *the* dealer — in Cancon and say I've got this stuff at home, will you come over and appraise my Layton collection. Here's his letter to me dated 23 October 1991.

To whom it may concern:

I have examined the attached list of books and periodicals by and concerning Irving Layton, and in my opinion, the fair market value of these items is $4,260.00.

Sincerely,

Stephen Temple

Now, I've been in lots of deals in my life, and you win some and lose some. I certainly had some good luck in TV; but nothing, nothing, comes close to the 1000x appreciation I've so far had on Irving's financial advice. The conclusion to be drawn from this seems to me, obvious.

Kick out that *poseur* Wilson and what's his name, the guy who came in after him, or that provincial clown who's got us ten billion dollars in the hole. I say, Irving Layton for Minister of Finance! I say, Irving Layton for Minister of Love, which this country sorely needs at this time . . . Hell, I say, Irving Layton for Prime Minister — apparently there will soon be an opening.

DEAR IRVING . . .

Musia Schwartz

Dear Irving,

When I recall our marathon talks in various campus-neighbouring cafes, during long walks, or at the kitchen table, I am amazed at the amount of things we shied away from saying or, on rare occasions, almost said.

Few people would believe that you and I could be self-consciously tongue-tied or embarrassed about sounding maudlin. And yet, the truth is, we were.

Now it's your eightieth birthday and the forty-something anniversary of our friendship. Time to reminisce, to smile at the host of memories, and above all, time to "officially" declare that I consider you the most inspiring and generous teacher, my most significant mentor, kindred spirit, and dear, dear, invaluable friend.

The extent of guidance and encouragement I received from you through the years is too enormous to be fit into words. It fits where it rightfully belongs, in my heart. There it's writ large.

How well I remember our first encounter. I had arrived in Canada about a year earlier. I was excited and intimidated by this new place, the journey's end which was fated to become my real home at last. Assailed by new sounds and sights which flooded my mind, and frustrated by the inability to translate them adequately into words, I was overwhelmed and at times discouraged. The rollercoaster of the unfamiliar was invigorating and vital, but it did not silence the need for the known, the familiar. The sound of a language which pleased rather than challenged. A book which could be read without a dictionary. People who needed no glossary when asked, "how did you survive?"

The closest thing to a haven providing the answer to such longings in 1948, was the Jewish Public Library on Esplanade Avenue. With its multilingual books and polyglot "regulars," it was a patch of the past, a temporary security blanket for the Europe-wrecked refugees.

It was Rachel Eisenberg, one of the library's pillars, who suggested and insisted that I sign up for your course of English Poetry, aimed at newcomers. She extolled your talents, ability and your exceptional enthusiasm. Still, I was sceptical. What was the use of listening to poetry, I asked myself, when the radio news often eluded me and conversation involving language a notch above basic English demanded head-splitting concentration.

Anticipating frustration and defeat, I went to your first class. You read poems and watched us intensely. Your eyes moved slowly around the table, looking into each face, searching. You seemed to intuit our uncertainties, guess our unspoken questions, because your perceptions were remarkably acute, your comments sensitive and accurate. We were stunned. "Is he really Canadian?" we whispered to each other. "How can he understand us so well? How can he possibly know how we feel?" My initial distrust began to show cracks at the end of the first class. I was hooked.

This was not teaching and learning in the ordinary sense. You read lines with such contagious affection and delight that you seemed to toss them to us, a gift, and we caught them, enchanted. I listened to you with reverence but dared not say a word.

Remember, Irving, when during the break, intrigued by peals of laughter in our corner, you asked if I would share the joke with you. You were obviously curious and eager to strike up a conversation. "It's nothing, it's nothing," I mumbled.

My lack of responsiveness in view of your prodigious appeal and popularity with students (female particularly) surprised and puzzled you. Years later, recalling the silly incident, you asked reproachfully, "why didn't you talk to me then? Couldn't you say boo?" (Of course, I more than made up for this uncharacteristic reticence, since.)

And do you remember Bardini, whose English at the time was no better than my own, reading "She Dwelt Among the Untrodden Ways?" We all held our breaths in humble silence, and when he reached the last stanza — "and, oh, / The difference to me!" — your eyes filled with tears, and you said with a tremor in your voice, "this was so beautiful," and shook his hand with admiration.

Not many of them would show up at a class reunion, I guess, but the ones I meet occasionally have not forgotten this unusual course, nor your warm concern and empathy for them. I missed the weekly meetings when the course ended and regretted never having talked to you. But a period of significant events took over my life and endowed it with another kind of poetry. I married Leon whom I met in your class, a fact which bestows upon you the out-of-character role of matchmaker. I had my children, Susan, then Robert, two unique blessings, and became fully immersed in the radiant joy of motherhood.

I followed your career, though. Your TV appearances on "Fighting Words" and even some piquant trivia which surrounded your flamboyant personal life.

Then one day, when adolescence, of which the war had cheated me, asserted its rights and directed my steps toward the academe, you and I met again. This time it was Sir George Williams College, on Drummond Street.

My English vocabulary had somewhat improved, and I was involved in writing a diary recalling my wartime experiences. You asked to read it. I was timid, full of doubt, conventional. You were exuberant, expansive, deriding convention. With "fear and trembling" I handed you an instalment. The following week you returned it wrapped in starlight and magic. You praised, encouraged and urged me to "unlock," to "be myself," to test and explore the roads "less travelled by." Your acclaim was overwhelming.

Thank God for my common sense which prevented me from being totally mesmerized by your hyperboles, but thank you for what they did for my self-esteem.

For better or for worse, Irving, you are singularly responsible for my enrolment in the Literature department. Our everlasting discussions (also disputes), your insights, your instant grasp of a literary work's depth and horizon, never ceased to amaze me. It was a perpetual, joyful seminar, Irving.

I had a chance to watch you in class at Sir George Williams. Your generous tolerance and yes, humility toward your students, showed me more about teaching than volumes of methodology. No comment or question raised by a student was ever too trivial or obtuse. "Yes, very good," your remarks began usually, then added "but there is also X and Y etc. you may want to look at," and so you guided without hectoring.

Later when I was the teacher and found myself tempted by impatience to snap at a less than brilliant student, a censoring voice

"Irving never would . . ." occasionally saved me from thoughtless, inglorious conduct.

Years have passed since that memorable poetry course at the Jewish Public Library. Years which added depth, richness and warmth to my life and the lives of my family. Our unparalleled friendship is a gift as bountiful as it is rare.

Dear Irving, friend, teacher, poet, beautiful heart, with affection and gratitude, I salute you.

Musia

Teaching at Sir George Williams College, ca. 1957.
Courtesy of Irving and Anna Layton.

ON MEETING IRVING LAYTON

Joy Bennett

In 1972 I had just returned to Montreal from a year in Paris and was looking for a job. With an undergraduate degree in English Literature and all but one course completed for an M.A. in the same discipline, my prospects were not the best. One day I received a telephone call from James Polson, the Head of the Reference department at Concordia University Library. He asked me if I was interested in a part-time job as a research assistant, and explained that the job entailed cataloguing and arranging the Irving Layton collection. At that time my knowledge of Irving Layton and his poetry was minimal. The focus of my education had been sixteenth and seventeenth century British poetry and drama. I had never taken a single Canadian literature course, much less actually studied Layton's work. For some reason Polson didn't seem too concerned with my lack of knowledge of the subject and when I said "yes," he hired me.

For the next ten months I sorted through boxes of clippings, correspondence, manuscripts, photographs, laundry lists, airline tickets and whatever else had been deposited in what came to be called the Irving Layton Collection. Most of the time I worked alone in a secluded office, surrounded by the boxes of assorted correspondence, piles of newspaper clippings, and an overflowing shoe-box of file cards, with only occasional visits from Polson to see how I was doing.

In fact, I was hooked. Hooked on the life and letters and poetry of this incredible and fascinating man. I became compulsive about elusive references to Layton or his work and was determined to make the collection as complete and accurate as possible. I learned to identify the type face of most major Canadian newspapers so that I could identify and date clippings, I studied the handwriting of his various correspondents so that at a glance I could identify a letter from Desmond Pacey, Jonathan Williams or Steve Osterlund. I visited the MacDonald College Library to search for copies of the

Failt-Ye Times in which Layton had published some of his earliest poems and political thoughts.

One day, during the summer of 1973, I was working in my office when I heard a commotion in the main office area. Someone was looking for Jim Polson and seemed to be quite distressed that Polson could not be found. I went out to see if I could help and was faced with a rather short, stocky man, carrying a canvas gym bag, who announced that he was Irving Layton and that he had some "goodies" for the Layton Collection. After I had properly introduced myself, Layton proceeded to open his rather shabby gym bag and handed me several manuscripts, some letters and a pile of newspaper clippings. Thus began my long and interesting relationship with Irving Layton.

My own friendship with Irving took on an added dimension in 1991 when I went to Romania, his birth land, to adopt a baby. My daughter, Marian Caroline, is now nearly two years old, and I am proud that she shares a rich heritage with our gifted poet. Irving Layton's present to her, to mark her safe arrival in Canada, and the beginning of her life with us, was, fittingly, a poem.

JOY BENNETT

Song for Marian

I too watch my daughter
playing in the tall grasses,
sturdy legs and arms golden
in the afternoon sunlight,
the confident tilt of her dark head
affirming life.

A tiny survivor, entrusted to me
by a strife ravaged country
where infants are a luxury.

She shares a rich Romanian heritage
with that other daughter seen
"singing in the grasses so tall"
by her poet father.

She sees me watching and points
to flower, berry and butterfly
and queries in her infant tongue, "dis?"
I give her words to make sense
of her world and the love to endure it.
Her heritage and time will do the rest.

CONTRIBUTORS

DOUG BEARDSLEY is a writer and poet. He teaches English at the University of Victoria and is the editor of *The Rocket, the Flower, the Hammer and Me* (1988).

HENRY BEISSEL is a poet, playwright, and translator, who teaches literature and Creative Writing in the English Department of Concordia University. Author of over twenty books, he also published and edited the literary journal, *Edge*. In collaboration with the composer Wolfgang Bottenberg he has written the libretto for an opera based on his successful play, *Inook and the Sun*, which premièred in Stratford in 1973. His most recent publications are *The Noose & Improvisations for Mister X* (plays, 1990), *Dying I Was Born* (poems, 1992), and *Stones to Harvest* (poems, 1993).

JOY BENNETT was appointed to the Concordia University Library in 1976, and until the present year has been responsible for the Irving Layton Collection. Her publications on Irving Layton include: *Irving Layton: A Bibliography 1935–1977* (1981); *A Catalogue of the Manuscripts in the Irving Layton Collection, Concordia University* (1988); and *A Catalogue of the Letters, Tapes and Photographs in the Irving Layton Collection, Concordia University* (at press). She is currently Associate Vice-rector, Institutional Relations and Finance at Concordia University.

PER BRASK teaches theatre and drama at the University of Winnipeg. He is the co-author (with George Szanto) of *Duets* (1989).

VALERIO BRUNI is an Italian writer and critic.

MERVIN BUTOVSKY teaches English at Concordia University. He is co-editor and translator of *Jacob Zipper, The Far Side of the River: Selected Short Stories*, and co-editor of *An Everyday Miracle: Yiddish Culture in Montreal* (1990).

ELSPETH CAMERON teaches English at the University of Toronto. She is the author of *Irving Layton: A Portrait*.

NICHOLAS CATANOY, a Romanian writer and editor, edited *Modern Romanian Writing* (1977; foreword by Irving Layton).

FRED COGSWELL is the author of *Immortal Plowman* and *Pearls*. He was editor of *The Fiddlehead* (1952–1967) and founder of Fiddlehead Books.

JOHN ROBERT COLOMBO is the creator of *Colombo's Canadian Quotations* and *Colombo's Canadian References*; only two examples of his essential Canadian compilations.

ROBERT CREELEY taught at Black Mountain College (North Carolina) in the 1950s at the invitation of fellow poet Charles Olson, and became editor of the influential *Black Mountain Review*.

ANN DIAMOND is a Montreal poet and fiction writer. Her most recent poetry collection is *Terrorist Letters* (1992).

EKBERT FAAS teaches English at York University. He edited, with Sabrina Reed, *Irving Layton and Robert Creeley: The Complete Correspondence 1953–1978* (1990).

WYNNE FRANCIS is retired from Concordia University where she taught Canadian and American literature. She is the author of *Irving Layton and His Works* (1984), and editor of *Irving Layton: Selected Poems* (1974).

JOYCE DAWE FRIEDMAN is a friend and former student of Irving Layton.

KEITH GAREBIAN is a critic and writer who teaches English at a Toronto high school and also teaches part-time at Trent University.

GARY GEDDES is a poet who teaches English and Creative Writing at Concordia University. His publications include *Terracotta Army* (1984), *Letters from Managua* (1990), and *Light of Burning Towers: Poems New and Selected* (1990).

WILLIAM GOODWIN is Irving Layton's cousin and teaches English at one of the Montreal CEGEPs.

RALPH GUSTAFSON is winner of the Governor-General's Award for Poetry. His most recent book is *Configurations at Midnight* (1992).

SHARON KATZ is a visual artist who lives and works in Ottawa. She has exhibited nationally and internationally and her work is held in many public, corporate, and private collections.

VENERANDA KREIPANS-MCGRATH is a former student of Layton's who teaches English at a Montreal secondary school.

BERNICE LEVER is a poet who teaches English at Seneca College. She is the editor of *Singing*, an anthology of women's writing from Canadian prisons.

DOUGLAS LOCHHEAD is a poet and editor. He teaches English at Mt. Allison University. He is the author of *Upper Cape Poems*.

ROY MACSKIMMING is a poet, novelist, and non-fiction writer. He is also Policy Director for the Association of Canadian Publishers.

SEYMOUR MAYNE is a poet, translator, and critic who teaches at the University of Ottawa. He is the author of *Children of Abel*, and most recently, *Killing Time* (1992).

JACK MCCLELLAND is the former president of McClelland and Stewart.

DOROTHY RATH is a longtime friend and admirer of Layton. She is the editor of *An Unlikely Affair* (1980), the correspondence between Layton and herself.

ALFREDO RIZZARDI is the author of *Canada: The Verbal Creation (La creazione verbale)* (1985).

NANCY-GAY ROTSTEIN is a lawyer and writer. She is the author of *China: Shockwaves* (1987).

THEODORE SAMPSON teaches American and Commonwealth literature at the University of Athens, Greece. His publications include *Five Canadian Poets in Greece* (1972), Modern Greek Short Stories (1980), and an English translation of Petros Haris' *The Longest Night* (1985).

FRUMA ROTHBERG SANDERS is a Montreal artist whose work has been included in *Chronicles of Canada*.

MUSIA SCHWARTZ is a friend and former student of Irving Layton. She has taught English in the Montreal area.

DAVID SOLWAY won the QSPELL Poetry Prize for *Modern Marriage* and QSPELL Non-Fiction Prize for *Education Lost*. His most recent book is *The Anatomy of Arcadia* (1992). He teaches English at John Abbott College.

RICHARD SOMMER teaches English and Creative Writing at Concordia University. His most recent book is *The Shadow Sonnets*.

RAYMOND SOUSTER, co-publisher of the seminal Contact Press, edited the literary magazines, *Contact* and *Combustion*. His most recent book is *Asking for More* (1988). He won the 1964 Governor-General's Award for Poetry.

SHULA STEINBERG was a student of Irving Layton's at Herzliah High School in the 1950s.

MARIA TROMBACCO is collaborating with Ekbert Faas on a biography of American poet Robert Creeley.

ANDY WAINWRIGHT is a poet who teaches English at Dalhousie University. He is the author of *The Requiem Journals* (1976).

GEORGE WOODCOCK, essayist and poet, is the author of *Crystal Spirit* which won the 1966 Governor-General's Award, and *Beyond the Blue Mountains* (1985). He was founding editor of the literary periodical, *Canadian Literature*.

KIM YANG-SHIK is a Korean poet and essayist. She is president of the Tagore Society of Korea.

MOSES ZNAIMER is a former student of Layton's and is president of CITY-TV.

DATE DUE